Deliverance through Buddhism

(Buddhist concepts that illuminate Life's Journey)

(Part I)

by

Dayaratne Ranasinghe

(Translation of the Book " NIVANA ")

Dayaratne Ranasinghe

ISBN : 955 - 95611 - 3 - 8

First Edition
September 1995

Copyright is reserved

Printed by :

Tharanjee Prints,
506, Highlevel Road,
Nawinna - Maharagama.
Tel : 854773

English Translation
by
L. M .V. de Silva

Dedication

This volume is dedicated reverently to the memory
of my dear parents
who fondly brought me up in the ways
of righteous living and also to my much revered
Guru-deva, Maha Thera, Agga Maha Pandita,
Balangoda Ananda Maitreya
of Bosat Qualities whose lotus feet
I worship with profound humility.

Quotations

From Anguttara-Nikaya "The Book of the Ones"

" No other thing do I know, O Monks that brings so much harm as a mind that is untamed, unguarded, unprotected, and uncontrolled.
 Such a mind, indeed, brings much harm. "

" No other thing do I know, O Monks, that brings so much benefit as a mind that is tamed, guarded, protected and controlled.
 Such a mind, indeed, brings great benefit. "

" Luminous, O Monks, is the mind :
 And it is defiled by adventitious defilements. "

" Luminous, O Monks, is the mind :
 And it is free from adventitious defilements. "

FOREWORD

In the present time there have been many books published in English and Other Western languages, that deal with various systems of meditation and mind culture. It is noticed that some books and other publications have appeared in Sinhala as well. These publications no doubt, have contributed towards the appreciation of Buddhist ideals. But I think a correct explanation is necessary here. Many of the aforesaid publications on meditation and other forms of yogic practices have been compiled with direct reference and dependence on the ancient treaties that have been written mainly in the Pali and Sanskrit languages. Many of these new publications do not reveal practical and personal experiences of persons who have engaged themselves in direct meditational practices. As such some of the expositions undertaken in these publications do seem to lead the reader astray. Some publications have as their only aim, the creation of a successful business enterprise. These undoubtedly lead to disservice than service.

I am personally known to Dayaratne Ranasinghe the author of this volume. I am aware of the fact that he has personally engaged in meditational practices and attained quite a high degree in mental poise and mind culture. He is even at present engaged constantly in exercises dealing with high meditation. A book on meditational practices published by such a person, is primarily based on his personal experience gained in direct meditational practices. As such, the instructions that have been given in this book, would be very helpful to those interested in meditational practices.

Balangoda Ananda Maitreya Maha Thero.

1993.09.04

Note from the Translator

When I was asked to translate Dayaratne Ranasinghe's "Nivana" into English, I was rather hesitant to undertake this task, because I felt that I would soon get into deep waters in trying to put into English the deep and highly spiritual concepts of Bhavana or Meditation. Therefore, I had to read the book many times over in order to correctly apprise myself of the intentions and flow of thought developed, by the author.

The simple Sinhala style that the author had adopted in writing this series soon encouraged me. The deep concepts of meditation were being presented in a direct and simple form. Hence, I decided to follow the same simple style that had characterised the original book.

I must add a personal note. I attempted this translation with a sense of veneration for the 'Buddha Dhamma' that had influenced me deeply even from childhood. The pali terms have been sparingly used and always at first appearance, the English equivalent was given.

This book, as the author himself had stated is for the beginner. Hence, it is hoped that the general English public would be interested in this simple translation.

L. M. V. de Silva

40/5, Mission Road,
Kotte.

Introduction

The greatest benefit that I derived by engaging in meditational exercises, was the realisation that I was a very ignorant person. When I realised this fact, it was possible for me to engage earnestly in search of the final truth manifest in the universe. It became then possible for me to understand the basic and fundamental concepts of truth or to put it in a different way to understand the "suchness" in the universe. When one contemplates on the manifold concepts of this universal truth, the realisation dawns as to how infinitely small is the degree of what all had come to be realised. Till an individual is able to reach supreme enlightenment, until that time, how infinitely small would one be to understand the manifold secrets that are so intricately manifest in this wide universal system.

When I was engaged in this search after truth according to the concepts of Buddhism, my inner self began to be filled with an immense joy when even a very minute concept of truth became clear to my mind. The joy derived from such a situation cannot easily be described. This satisfaction egged me on to further effort towards deeper realisation. I can well imagine the concept of ultimate freedom that would arise from a truly and fully liberated mind.

This volume is the result of an effort made by me to convey to the vast multitudes of suffering individuals, what joy and happiness is inherent in such meditational practices. I was able to do this as I had gained some experience as a journalist, and therefore, through the medium of the Sunday Edition of the "Divaina" I was able to publish a series of articles entitled "Buddhist concepts that illuminate life's journey".

The question may be asked why such a simple type of writing was made use in these articles to express such a deep philosophy as Buddhism. My intention in using such a direct and simple style was to open the door as it were, to even to the most uninitiated who could then be led gently towards final liberation. The disciplines that I had gathered as a journalist, helped me in great measure to put across these difficult concepts in simple and direct terms as possible.

To the question that was asked "on what is the world established?" the Tathagata answered directly that the world was established on Dukkha or suffering. The main and fundamental intention of these articles was to make the great truth go deep down into the minds and hearts of those individuals whose vision is covered by a deep veil of ignorance. If after reading this book, there is implanted in the mind of the reader a certain concept of fear and uneasiness about the long sansaric journey, that would be satisfaction enough for me. I say this because when this sansaric fear has once arisen, then at some time or other however distant it may be, that fear would result in the final liberation of the mind.

On a personal note the demise of five young brothers and more especially the death of a sister at her prime of life, due to excessive bleeding resultant in child birth, made such a deep impression on me, that I was constantly assailed by the fear of impending death and disaster. This unnatural fear was so persistent that it was only after meditational exercises, that I was able to cure myself of this mental aberation.

In trying to explain lucidly the basic concepts of meditation, I am humble enough to accept any errors that may have crept into it. But I have always attempted not to deviate from the basic tenets of the Buddha Dhamma. Many instances that I have expounded here, are not necessarily found in the Texts of Buddhism. There are instances that have been brought forward after I have thought deeply on them, and thus realised their fundamental truth. I have attempted to wean the general public, especially the youth, of the entanglement of greed and commercialism, towards understanding the mind liberating concepts of Scientific Buddhism. It is the Lord Buddha's exhortation to 'travel far and wide and spread the doctrine for the good and benefit of the many' had been a guiding force that pushed me to continuously write these series.

What has been attempted here is to explain clearly experiences that I had deeply felt during meditational practices and not merely those expositions found in the accepted Texts. Hence there may be certain discrepansies with accepted concepts and beliefs. As an example I would refer to the chapter where certain observations have been made on the intermediate stage after death, normally called 'Anthara Bhava'. Most of the views have been consequent to the clear concepts felt intensely in Meditation. The views of Indian and Tibetan sages and Western scholars too have been taken into consideration. For those interested on this subject, the reference made by the Buddha, in the Salayatana Vagga of the Sanyutta Nikaya would be helpful. Insidently, the Late Ven, Pandit Henpitagedera Gnanaseha Maha Thero too has expressed views on this controversial topic. I am happy to state that I too totally agree with the views expressed by the late Maha Thero. It must be stated however that this view was not accepted by me earlier, but after the experience I had gathered after Meditation. I must honestly say again that I fully accept the view as expressed by the Late Maha Thero.

In the classical explanation of the concept of "Patichcha Samuppada" or Dependent causation, the term Upadana leads to Bhava and this leads to Jati or Re-birth. I am of the opinion that the term 'Bhava' should be interpreted as 'Anthara Bhava' or the Intermediate State mentioned earlier. In these series of articles I have purposely left out intricate quotations from the Original Texts, as such quotations would divert ones attention from the main Points explained here. It has to be noted that the main intention of these articles is to make the reader realise the Dhamma. There is no intention at all of expounding a learned Text on Buddhist Philosophy.

In the earlier articles I have very purposely adopted a very simple style of exposition, and emphasis on the worldly benefits of meditation in order to interest the reader to further perusing of the articles and thus kindle the interest on meditation.

After these articles were published in the Newspapers, the greatest satisfaction I derived was when many non-Buddhists came to see me personally and discussed various concepts that had been explained in these articles. They wanted clarification, and the discussion gave me much satisfaction. There were also a flood of letters I received from those who were interested in learning the Dhamma. I was extremely happy that among the category were a large number of young people who were very keen to understand the Dhamma. I must add that there were very abusive letters too, which I decided to ignore.

Finally I must pay my respects again to the Ven. Agga Maha Panditha Ananda Maitreya Maha Thero for the encouragement he persistently gave me towards writing these articles in the "Divayina" paper. When often I was somewhat discouraged by the unsympathetic and unfair critisism that I received from some quarters, it was his sincere encouragement that speared me on. His suggestions were always very sincere and timely and contributed much towards making the articles more readable and much more meaningful.

I am particularly thankful to the Chairperson of the Upali Newspapers Ltd, Mrs. Lakmani Wijewardena Welgama for all the encouragement, and to the Editorial Staff and all connected with this Institution for the great interest shown.

It is my earnest hope that those who read this series would be able to use them as a raft to cross the ocean of Sansara.

Dayaratne Ranasinghe

No. 1/68, 1st Lane,
Meda Welikada Road,
Rajagiriya,
Sri Lanka.
1993.11.25

CONTENTS

		Page No.
01.	Illumination through meditation	01 - 09
02.	Why should we meditate?	10 - 13
03.	The mind and cosmic energy	14 - 19
04.	The Karmic Force that connects an individual to the universal cosmic energy	20 - 27
05.	The manner in which Karma results manifest	28 - 36
06.	The dark tissues that lengthen the Sansaric Journey	37 - 45
07.	The long and fearful Sansaric Journey	46 - 52
08.	Cosmic travel is regulated by gravity while Thanha or greed activates the Journey In Sansara	53 - 63
09.	Is there a permanent soul that travels in Sansara or Round of re-birth?	64 - 78
10.	We are one Family In Sansara	79 - 86
11.	In the Sansaric Journey, earthly sojourn is a place of rest, a university and also it is a great fair	87 - 96
12.	It is possible for an artistically inclined child to be forced into medical studies?	97 - 104
13.	I am my own enemy	105 - 112
14.	" Do you love yourself "	113 - 118
15.	The Newtonial Principles which the Buddha explained 2500 years ago	119 - 123

CONTENTS

                                                  Page No.

16. Committing suicide is like drinking molten liquid to quench one's thirst   124 - 132

17. Those who weep and lament at death - are they the ones that do not die?   133 - 140

18. Illumination that dawns from understanding the concept of death   141 - 148

19. Dying unconscious and arising of the last thought process   149 - 155

20. Getting caught in enemy traps and drinking molten - lava   156 - 162

21. At the moment of death, is it light or darkness that is experienced?   163 - 170

22. Relatives who often harm the departed   171 - 178

23. The janaka - citta or impulsive thought process that is generated at death caused by a time bomb.   179 - 191

24. The Antara - Bhavika who drift towards animal existence while in sight of the hellish regions   192 - 200

CHAPTER I

Illumination through meditation

The purpose of this article is to explain to the layman the benefits that would accrue, through the practice of meditation or bhavana. If one, were to accept the fact, that meditative practice is the foundation on which a Buddhist way of life can be built and developed, then I would wish to explain to the lay reader in simple terms as possible the varied experiences that I have personally undergone by the continuous practice of meditative exercises.

May I say at the very beginning that meditative exercises cannot be undertaken in a haphazard manner. As these exercises attempt to bring about a semblance of order to an otherwise distorted mind, the instrument of such control being the mind itself, the methods adopted must be done carefully and correctly. I am aware of many instances of those who had attempted meditative practices in an incorrect manner which had resulted in leading the aspirant to very distorted mental conditions. As the mind reacts to various stimuli in a much more effective manner than any other human organ, steps taken towards the control of the mind that diffuses itself instantly must be done, in a very careful manner.

It is difficult to exactly specify the dawn of the human species on the planet earth. According to evolutionary concepts humanoids would have appeared on earth resultant to a process of change that had started to occur at a vastly distant date of many millions and millions of years. The consciousness of such a being that had been subjected by the manifold process of change during the long expanse of time of many millenniums would have resulted in the acquisition of such energies absolutely necessary for a vastly long sansaric journey.

I would prefer to name such energies as Karmic Flux.

The primary aim of the meditational process is to clear the mind in order to get a clear concept of Nirvana. By Nirvana is meant the final stop that is put to a beings travel in the great ocean of Sansara. Mind or consciousness that had gone through immensely long periods of time of constant becoming and breaking up and becoming again only to break up again, this process lasting aeons and Kalpas and in such a process the mind had acquired to itself certain habits, likes, dislikes and defilements. I would there fore like to define Bhavana as an instrument by which the above condition of the mind that had become almost second nature be transferred into something positive.,

The mind that had existed and changed, developed through myriads of years, in a particular manner, cannot be altered in a short space of a day or two. The reaction of the mind to such an attempted change would certainly be negative and serious. May we look at this problem in a different manner? What would be easier for the mind? To do something that is accepted generally as good and positive, or to do something quite opposite. To attempt a good or positive deed will have to be done with some effort and determination, while a negative or bad action could be performed effortlessly. The Tathagatha the perfect one has fully expounded the evil proclivities of greed, anger and ignorance that are rooted in the human mind. The concept of the five hindrances or Pancha Nivarana Dhamma have been explicitly enumerated. As such it is not necessary at present to explain and further clarify these concepts.

A beginner in the field of meditation should have at least an elementary knowledge regarding the workings of the mind, and hence it is my intention to give an explanation of it in a most simple manner as possible. It has to be accepted that the mind does not rest in one place at every moment, that it is easily diffused and travels as far as it so desires. What are we attempting to do to this ever-changing ever-diffusing mind when we try our first steps in meditation? Our attempt at such a moment to fix the mind on a certain point is to tie it up as it were, and thus to tame the ever restless mind.

It is equivalent to an attempt made by a hunter to capture a wild elephant that roams freely in a herd, and thus tame it to better ways. This elephant has been used to roam freely eating at leisure and doing what it desires without obstruction. One could imagine the result that would arise when such an elephant had been noosed and tied up so that by and by it could be tamed. The noosed elephant would use all its strength to break free and gain its freedom. It has to be tamed by a process of limited feeding for a period of months and even in some instances of being physically beaten by other tame elephants, so that in the course of time it would change these habits, give up its wild ways and get used to a newer environment. Such a process of taming would take quite a period of time. The taming of the mind would also be similar. When at the beginning a novice engages himself to practice even the elementary stages of whatever form of meditation, such a person would experience a greater sense of agitation than earlier. He would easily lose his temper and be agitated. This condition is common to anyone who starts to practise 'In and out breathing ' or contemplating on loving kindness, or any other form of meditation that is attempted.

This is due to the fact that the mind, like the wild elephant, would make every atempt to release itself from the bonds that are being imposed by Bhavana or meditation. It would show reluctance at the attempts made to bind it and bring it under control. There are ways of avoiding such a condition. In the beginning it would be best if meditation exercises are limited to a very short period of time. When one attempts daily to meditate for short periods, the mind would naturally get used to such a situation and the agitation and resentment would gradually pass away. At this stage, without going into a detailed discussion as to how meditational exercises must be attempted, which I would leave for a later occasion, I would like to enumerate certain conditions that would appear which would certainly lead the aspirant astray.

* Development of a sense of superiority in himself.

* Sees a halo around him. Thinks he can perform supernatural feats, and has such special powers, and attempts to tread different paths.

* Imagines that he has a protective force working around him.

* Believes he could read the minds of others.

* That he could see hidden objects with his mind's eye and appearance of such distorted views.

* Development of a sense of unnatural disgust and disap pointment about the condition of the world especially among immature aspirants who have attempted deep meditational practices without guidance of a competent teacher, leading to a distorted mind.

* Describing in exaggerated terms the excellence of medi tative systems, to everyone whom he meets and speaks to, without descrimination,.

The above list enumerates some aspects of distortion that may arise in a person who attempts meditational exercises in an incorrect manner.

Let us discuss these matters in greater detail. If at the beginning one were to engage in meditational practices with over enthusiastic energy, and great strain there would arise not an attitude of compassion but one of resentment and anger. He would soon get angry even for a trivial cause.

The question would naturally arise how anger would arise in a person attempting the meditation of loving kindness or Metta. Such a situation would arise not because of the topic of meditation, but as the mind had been forced to engage itself for a long period of time on a single topic which would be most tiring and exacting. The anger and resentment would be the mind's reaction to a long and exhaustive exercise in focussing the mind.

How does a sense of superiority arise in a novice? There is a mistaken tendency among beginners to feel that as one who engages in meditational practices, one is a superior individual, and all those who do not practise these methods are inferior. One meditates and hence one is superior. Others do not, and hence they are of a lower status. These attitudes are common features in the minds of a worldling or potujjana. That such thoughts are de-meritorious or Akusala Citta eventually arise in the meditators mind.

There is quite a possibility for a beginner to proceed on wrong tracks and to do great harm to himself and fall into deep pitfalls. One engages in meditational practices not to achieve the aforesaid wrong targets. Many proceed on the wrong tracks due to the absence of guidance of a competent teacher. It is important that a beginner in meditational practices should be aware of the pitfalls quite early. Then he could avoid them and avoid the unpleasant consequences that would inevitably befall him. Avoiding these dangers he would then be able to proceed correctly and derive great benefit.

Let us explain how even among daily household activities the in-and-out breathing meditational practices could be attempted. It is necessary to select a quiet and restful environment at first. There should be sufficient ventilation and the surroundings be peaceful.

The posture for meditation should be correctly chosen. It is essential that one must be seated with the spine quite straight. If it is more convenient to lean against a wall there should not be any serious objections to it as long as the spine is kept quite straight. If sitting cross-legged on the ground is inconvenient, sitting on a low chair could be attempted. Sitting uncomfortably should be avoided as a painful sitting posture would be detrimental to meditational exercises. If one is quite comfortable sitting on the floor with crossed legs such a posture would be ideal. What is most important is to keep the body straight and without sagging. The eyes should be directed towards the tip of the nose. The eyelids should be lightly closed.

The inflow and outflow of the breath should be mentally noticed without any forced attempt. This exercise can be attempted in two ways. The mind should be directed to notice the striking of the in breath at the tip of the nose, and the expansion of the stomach and secondly the exit of the breath as it strikes the tip of the nose and the consequent deflation of the stomach.

It is also possible to fix ones awareness on the spot where the breath strikes on in-breathing and also the spot the breath strikes in out-breathing. The mind should be directed towards the tip of the nose where the breath strikes and towards the inflation and deflation of the stomach. When one practices this exercise for some time the time would arise when one would not be conscious of the existence of a body but only be aware of the inflow and outflow of breath as it strikes the tip of the nose. Or one would be conscious only of the expansion and deflation of the stomach.

To a novice who practices in-and-out-breathing, during the early days, the tendency would be prevalent to take in and send out the breath with an effort, and with purpose. This purposeful breathing in and out is adopted as a means to tie down the mind as there would be a tendency for the mind to wander. In and out breathing should not be attempted purposely and forcibly. One should concentrate on the natural and effortless in-flow and outflow of the breath.

When engaged in the meditational exercise of in and out breathing, sometimes it so occurs that the mind will deviate from the exercise and try to move in other directions. When this happens it is best to stop the exercise for a little while, and to follow the path of the mind. If one were to engage in the meditational exercise in a strained manner, the tendency of the mind would then be to seek, various other objectives. When such a situation occurs it would be difficult to proceed effectively in meditation. When the meditator follows where the mind has deviated to, then the mind has the tendency to return back to its original topic. When this situation arises, the in and out breathing meditational process could be re-started.

It has been noticed that to some at the beginning of this exercise, it would be difficult to even concentrate for a short period of ten seconds at a time. The beginner would be discouraged and be dissapointed and would come to the conclusion that it would be impossible to bring some sort of order to an otherwise disoriented mind. He would then be discouraged to proceed any further.

Even in such situations of seemingly little progress one should not be discouraged. Then if one were to follow as to where the mind had deviated and recognised the deviation then it would become clear that the mind could not engage itself in any so called secret thinking of its own, without being made aware of such thought processes. When such thought processes are carefully followed up to their logical conclusions, then the mind's tendency for deviation and for disturbing thoughts to arise, will soon disappear.

On the first occasion engage in the meditated practices of the in-and-out breathing for a period about five minutes. In this way, the period of relaxed concentration could be expanded very gradually., When you have engaged yourself in this exercise for a considerable period of time, the process of inflation and deflation of the stomach and the contact of the in-going and out-going breath at the tip of the nose would become very clear in your mind and the awareness would become very keen. Then it would be possible for you to fix your mind on a particular place for a continuous period of two minutes. In such a situation you would experience great happiness. If you are able to concentrate your mind in such a manner for a period of even two to three minutes, you have progressed satisfactorily on the path of meditative practices.

This meditational exercise would soon make you realise the workings of your mind. When you have engaged yourself in these exercises for a considerable period of time, and so collected your mind and become reposed, you will realise even in an elementary form the knowledge of things as they are. Your wisdom and knowledge would see a marked improvement. You will gain self-confidence and self-trust.

Egoistic concepts will become less. Your capacity for forbearance and patience will develop., Even if you were to lose your temper, such tendencies will disappear soon. You would not take serious cognisance of the wrongs done to you by others, as you correctly understand universal laws. You would lightly treat the wrongs of others dismissing them as the way of the world. You would realise that the wrong had not been done by the individual, but by the evil proclivities that are found in him. When thoughts of jealousy and competition arise one would begin to realise the baneful influence of such thoughts to oneself, and how such thoughts would negate and destroy the positive characteristics. All these aspects would become very clear. If one were addicted to liquor and such harmful practices, this meditation practice would clearly indicate to him the baneful results that accrue to him. He would therefore avoid and give up such habits.

In addition to all these, 'In and out breathing ' meditation constantly practised would physically result in the fading away of psycho-somatic diseases. You would be able to face the vicissitudes of the world with calm and equanimity. You will not be mentally disturbed when problems assail you. You would develop a calm disposition, unruffled at all times.

Constant practices of the ana-pana, sati bhavana would result in granting you great illuminations of mind.

P.S In this article I have tried to explain the beneficial results that would accrue to a person leading a normal householders life. By constant development of this meditative practice one would be able to reach higher psychic states and develop 'Vipassana' by which one would be able to attain the transcendental states. I shall attempt to explain meditative practices that lead to such profound states in the future articles.

CHAPTER II

Why should we meditate ?

The question is often asked as to why a person should engage himself in meditational exercises. The answer to this question becomes very simple if we were to consider the normal every-day actions of life. Why does one wash the face and clean the teeth daily? Why are clothes washed often and on? Why are cups and saucers that have been used washed and cleaned? Why does one service a vehicle once in two or three months?

The answers to such questions are extremely simple. These activities are being done constantly in order to clean them and keep them in good order. If they are not cleaned they become dirty. Dust and dirt would collect in the course of time; not only would they be dirty, but the dirt would finally cause their destruction. This is the normal way of the world. What really happens is not mere destruction but a change from one condition to another; There is nothing in the whole universe, that completely destroys itself. If there were such a condition of total destruction, after a course of time everything that exists would be completely destroyed and there would be nothing left behind. This is another interesting question about which we shall discuss as we proceed, at a later time.

If tangible objects that are not cleaned become dirty, what happens to the mind that is intangible? This same process becomes manifest to the mind as well. If the mind is not cleaned, 'dirt' and 'dust' would collect and it would become quite greasy and dirty. There are five entrances in our body itself, through which dirt enters, and pollutes the original purity of the mind. These entrances or doors are termed as the five senses. They are termed as Eye, Ear, Tongue, Nose and Body. When an attractive sight, a pleasant sound, exciting taste or exquisite perfume, and soothing feeling assails, the mind cling to these stimuli steadfastly. Such a condition arises because of the greed that exists in the mind. We cling to these conditions in a most desperate manner. We do so because of the insatiable Tanha or greed that exists in us.

Why is it that it is so difficult to understand this condition? It is because of ignorance or Moha. What is ignorance or Moha? Is it foolishness? Foolishness conveys a narrow meaning. Moha or ignorance actually means the covering up or hiding of the truth-Satya-or the true condition of things as they really are. It can be compared to darkness. More than at any other time, there are at present conditions that tend to pollute and distort the mind. It therefore becomes most essential, that as much as we clean and polish and remove the dirt in the articles of our daily life, the mind too must be cleansed of the dirt and the grease that has covered its surface. What would be the result if this dirt is not removed?

More than any other object in the world the so called mind changes at very great speed. Most of the objects that the mind takes in are those that make it impure. As more and more of these impure thoughts gather in the mind, there forms as it were a thick layer of impurities. It can be compared to a gross outer layer. With the growth of the impure tendencies both the mind and the body need satisfaction according to the nature of these traits. This leads to insatiable desires of mind and body. This condition of the mind can be compared to the action of the moth, that jumps to the flame falsely believing the flame to be light. Needless to say that this brings total destruction to the moth.

It is interesting to find out as to what happens when a considerable amount of impurities gather in the mind. There appears a rough covering consisting of all those tendencies that have penetrated into the mind so far without the least resistance.

All the problems that confront the mind are passed through this impure covering to make this covering a protective barrier behind which it hides. It then arrives at a pre-conceived notion. As it tries to find answers to its problems through such pre-conceived decisions, the correct answers evade it. The true -picture of things as they really are get covered up. What one sees as answers are merely reflections of those pre-conceived ideas and not reality.

What happens at this point? One is engaged in self-deception. The answers he obtains for the everyday problems of life, all become evasions,. His so-called answers lead him to greater confusion. Finally he gets entangled in a mess of wrong views, which may lead him to a mental crisis and breakdown. He would seek temporary satisfaction from the problems by indulging in intoxicating liquor and drugs. As time goes on he would become an addict to such evils. Unknowingly, one would be destroying oneself.

What are the results that accrue from Meditation? Let us take a very simple example and try to understand this problem. Let us take the sun light that sustains life, as an example. The sun light falls to the earth in straight lines. As the rays spread evenly the temperature remains constant. If the sun's rays are concentrated and passed through a crystal, it would result in producing a great energy, through which fire can be generated.

The mind too acts in a similar manner. If it is possible to concentrate, the mind which hitherto had been widely diffused on various extraneous objects, the result would be almost the same. Then it would be possible to develop a great force, a great power, a great energy through the mind itself. Meditating is essential to develop the mind's power.

With the performance of constant exercises for the control of the mind, the time would not be too distant for the mind to bring about a semblance of order to the inflow of thoughts, that had previously flowed in at will and in a disorderly manner.

The mind will begin to have the strength to control the inflow of thoughts. With the development of this mental power it would be possible to recognise the thought processes, whether they are beneficial or otherwise. When this understanding dawns it would be possible for all to lead a beneficial life to themselves and also for the benefit of others.

When negative thoughts such as jealousy, anger, resentment and revenge appear, the mind would have to recognise them as such. It would be possible to clearly understand the baneful results that would inevitably follow, if these thoughts are allowed to establish themselves in the mind. It would be possible to protect oneself before one tries to protect others.

Meditational exercises would lessen to a very great extent the incidence of mental disturbances and mental disorders that are so common in modern society. Unnatural and imaginary fear that sometimes appear could be eradicated. It would be quite possible for one to find solutions to the manifold daily problems that would prop up from time to time, if one were to sit in quiet meditation for about half an hour daily. In addition, advice from a Meditation Master would be beneficial. Quite involuntarily as it were one would be developing tendencies and inclinations that would finally lead one away from the cycle of birth and death. One would realise how essential it is for one to spend even a limited period of time towards the perfection of meditational practices.

CHAPTER III

The mind and cosmic energy

How does the mind work? In order to understand easily the workings of the mind, let us pay attention as to how the universe is composed of . The universe is composed according to certain general laws. If the universe is taken as a unit every object that is in the universe also becomes part of the general law or pattern. Every part forms into the general pattern as it were.

Let us pay a little attention to the sky. The manifold stars and planets and other celestial objects are all spherical in shape. All these objects travel in space in circular or elliptical orbits. The earth revolves on its own axis and moves round the sun in a spherical orbit. All other planets too follow the patterns of travelling round the sun in circular orbits. Let us consider the movement of a comet. It too travels around the sun in such an orbit, taking many hundreds of years sometimes to complete its journey, but always keeping to its own course. This is the reason why we see the same comet appearing regularly after a definite period of time. A drop of water takes a circular shape when it falls on a particular spot. When a pebble is thrown onto the surface of the water, ripples spread out from the place of contact in concentric circles. Many fruits are also circular in shape.

I have given the aforesaid examples in order to emphasise that the mind too works according to certain accepted laws that are manifest in the universe. As in the universe the mind too moves out in circles. The earth revolving on its own axis, and revolution around the sun signifies the law of constant change.

The mind too that moves in such orbital fashion receives its impulses from manifold sources.

Various photographic impressions that are on a film move at great speed and form a composite image on the screen. In such manner the mind too moving in circular fashion at an unimaginable speed takes on various impulses and impressions. You are already aware of the fact that these various impressions enter the mind through five entrances or doors, These impressions like the two sides of a coin, vary, being both positive and negative and result in the constant interaction of both forces, good and bad, on the mind which transforms itself in action resulting in the quality these actions being meritorious or otherwise, good or bad, dark or luminous.

These resultant actions are know by various names. They may be termed as good or bad, Kusal or Akusal. Light or heavy, white or black or by any other such definition. The results of such actions are borne by the individual while in his Sansaric journey. This concept has been defined by the Buddha as the Eightfold Vicissitudes of Life or Astha Loka Dharma which are named as profit and loss, fame and ill-fame and so forth. At first the impressions that enter the mind come into operation take the form of a chakra. According to the manner in which manifold impressions enter the mind there arise as it were two sets of thought processes. To understand this condition in a simple manner, may I call one set of impressions as 'dark coloured' and the other set of impressions as 'bright coloured'. Certain thought processes that make a deep impact, move right down to the minds sub-conscious level are those that have been constantly practiced or those that have gone deep down to the sub-conscious level due to the very strong impact that had been experienced, at the moment the experiences arose.

When a stimuli arises, certain impressions that are so deposited in the sub-conscious state appear at the conscious level and transform themselves in to action. The mind at such a stage does not have the power to control those actions. Such uncontrollable tendencies are due to the ingrained concepts of greed, anger and ignorance that have established themselves firmly in the mind process.

The state of the conscious mind is always conditioned by the tendencies that have continuously influenced the sub-conscious mind. According to the stimuli that enter the mind, there arise in the conscious mind states of wholesome or unwholesome volition, Kusala Karma or Akusala Karma. A state of brightness or darkness arise accordingly. Demeritorious thoughts arise in the mind due to the unwholesome roots of greed, anger and ignorance- Loba, Dosa and Moha - that are deeply ingrained in the mind. These aspects of the mind are known as kilasas or impurities. These Kilesas are characterised by heaviness darkness and agitation. If a colour is said to signify these characteristics it would be 'blackness' or 'darkness'.

When meritorious thoughts enter the mind, the mind becomes buoyant, and elated. Virtue or sila brings forth conditions of order, happiness, contentment, illumination, lightness to the mind. These conditions are caused by the presence of wholesome roots of non- greed, non- anger and non- delusion. This condition is characterised by white or radiance. The above two aspects of the mind are so different to each other as day is to night.

When evil thoughts enter the mind constantly through the five doors of the body, the mind pre-dominantly becomes dark in colour. Darkness or confusion grows. When meritorious thoughts enter the mind, the radiance or luminosity of the mind increases. When dark thoughts or Akusal conditions predominate the mind and consciousness becomes enveloped in a film that is coarse and dark. Meritorious thoughts produce the opposite conditions.

It is interesting to see how these various conditions react in a person at a particular time. One individual feels happy, elated, buoyant when the positive or luminous impressions pervade the mind; he experiences a period of mental happiness. When the dark straits of the mind gain predominance, there is anger, resentment and allied unsettled conditions.

These conditions of the mind are termed as "moods"'. In common conversation among people we often hear statements such as 'How is the chief's mood today?' Would one be able to convince him to get him to accept one's views? These good or bad moods or conditions of the mind do not last for a long period, as such. These conditions change according to the pattern that the mind has been fashioned. A new set of conditions appear with time.

Let us consider the condition of a mental patient. If the patient had been subjected to periodical mental disturbances, and if the occasion and conditions of such attacks have been carefully recorded it would be seen that the attacks would become acute when similar conditions or occasions repeat themselves. What reason can be attributed to the re-occurrence? This is because consciousness travels according to the movements of a chakra or circle and the mind reacting to such a movement gets distorted when such conditions suitable for distortion appear. These changes affect the social structure according to certain established universal cosmic laws, a certain period of time proves very beneficial and pleasant. Another period proves very unpleasant and disappointing.

This condition is common to people, to families, to enterprises or even to dynasties. Taking the Indian example, the Moriya and Gupta dynasties showed their excellence at a particular time in the nations history. That was the golden period of their culture . Later, at a different point of time their disintegration occurred. These changes signify the general cosmic pattern of things that are manifest in the universe.

There is a generally accepted statement that 'History repeats itself'. This emphasises the fact that when a certain set of circumstances repeat themselves, similar conditions that appeared under such circumstances can be manifest in a similar manner or with little adjustment. As the cosmic movements in the universe take place in circles or chakras it seems natural in the cosmic setting for situations to repeat as and when similar conditions arise. As an individual too is a composite unit of the universe, changes that occur continuously in the universe, also find reaction in the human being.

We have digressed somewhat away from the subject as to how the mind works. Hence let us turn once more to the subject under discussion.

We said earlier that the minds working occurs according to the movements of a chakra or circle What happens to the mind when luminous (kusal) thoughts or meritorious thoughts enter? The luminosity of the mind increases. Then the dark aspects of the mind that had been caused by evil proclivities diminish little by little. It is to this state of mind that the term lessening of defilements is referred to. Meditation is necessary to expand the degree of luminosity of the mind. When a person engages himself in meditational exercises regularly, the dark film that had enclosed the mind, gets less intensified and the layer becomes thin and weak. Its coarseness is lessened.

With the development of meritorious thoughts or Kusal citta the dark layer does not completely disappear. Its intensity is lessened. The dark layer becomes less dark; becomes fine. It must be mentioned here that as long as there is a dark covering or a fine covering, the presence of whatever type of covering, it paves the way for the individual to continue his journey in Sansara. Meritorious actions and demeritorious actions, both cause to lengthen ones sansaric journey. But it must be stated that with the development of meritorious sankaras (Kusal) invariably the defilements that had collected in the mind become less intense and their power is reduced. Certain cells of the brain that had long been dormant become activated. Then wisdom dawns. The luminosity of the mind expands.

Why, do films of whatever character, so called dark or fine, form over the surface of the mind? It is because of the influx of impressions into the consciousness. As you are already aware the mind changes rapidly as it takes in these impressions. How then would it be possible to avoid the formation of whatever type of cover-dark or fine-by the mind? This condition would become possible when the mind ceases to take in impressions of whatever kind.

Why does the mind take on impressions as it wishes? The mind pursues after an impression because such impression pleases the mind and satisfies the mind. The mind gets attached to such impressions. The mind changes quickly and seeks new impressions. If the mind does not change rapidly, it would then be possible to control the mind and prevent it from taking an impression. When attempts are made to control the mind or to tie it up, it seeks to roam at will. What is the method by which this naturally wily mind can be brought under some restraint or control? It can be achieved by trying to concentrate the mind on a single object, without allowing it to diffuse itself. Concentration of the mind can be achieved only by meditation.

What is attempted in meditation is the concentration of the mind on a single object. The mind is thus controlled. When this occurs, whatever film that builds around, the mind, whether dark or luminous, disappears and fades away. It would then be possible to understand clearly and realise correctly the real condition of the world. The absolute truth becomes manifest. When one understands the real condition of things as they really are, then the attachment or strands or bands that tie a person to sansaric existence fall away and become non-existent. The mind reaches absolute purity, becomes resplendeut and pliable. The mind unites itself to the absolute cosmic energy that is manifest in the total universe. Such is Nirvana.

CHAPTER IV

The Karmic Force that connects an individual to the universal cosmic energy.

"Many types of crimes are commited in the world at the present time. There seems to be no end to homicides and sex offences. The daily papers are full with such accounts. The perpetrators of the crimes seem to get away scot-free. They seem to have a life of ease and comfort. It seems as if all misfortune come in the way of those who try to lead a normal and correct way of life. Would such a situation arise if there is a thing called Karma?"

Let us consider the concept of time. At what period of time did the universe come into being? When would be its end? Is there a "finiteness" to the universe. If one were to look up into the night sky one would see many millions of stars and other celestial objects. What are they? We know that these celestial objects that we see form part of many thousands of other galaxies similar to the galaxy in which our solar system is situated. Could an ordinary human mind comprehend and understand the final limits of such galaxies . There is infiniteness in space. There is infiniteness in time as well.

Who could exactly point at the time at which the individual entered the Sansaric circle? The commencement of our journey in Sansara seems infinite in time. The point of such origin is impossible to comprehend.

This journey in Sansara would continue in future for an immensely long period of time, consisting of millions and millions of births and deaths, until one is able to attain that supreme state of mind called Nirvana.

It becomes impossible to understand the extent of the total universe as it is also impossible to understand the total concept of time. Could we even minutely indicate space as it is in the total universe? If one were to compare the time span of an individual with the total time span of the universe, the individual life span would be even less than the "twinkling of an eye". We have become accustomed to look at the world while being confined to such an infinitely small and minute span of time.

What is the period of time that an individual would exist in the context of an infiniteness of space and infiniteness of time. If one were to live out the full span of life, it would be about a hundred years. It may even be 60 or 70 years. 40 or 50 years. Or it may be even less.

What is your understanding of the total sum of Karmic energy that a person had collected in that immensely long sansaric journey? Does the man whom you thought was leading a very happy and pleasant life really lead such a life? Are you aware of the various mental conditions that he experiences in his life? The man who lives while committing the most dastardly crimes, for how many thousands of times does he 'live and die' - mentally suffering great pains?

I went to the extent of explaining the above facts in order to stress the fact that any act or Karma performed at some point of time, would invariably produce results, however distant that day would be. When a seed is planted in the soil, and if there is sufficient water and fertility, in course of time the seed would become a plant. Time would elapse before the plant would put forth branches and leaves. A further period of time would elapse before the plant puts out flowers and fruits. Flowers and fruits would appear at different times according to the nature of its variety. If one were to consider the planting of a seed as the commencement of a Karma or action, the period of time of flowering and appearance of fruits can be termed as the result or Vipaka of the earlier Karma of planting the seed.

Let us take for example the progress of a disease. When a disease-causing germ enters the body, it so happens that sometimes the disease manifests itself almost immediately. It is also possible that the same germ or any other germs may enter the body and remain for an year or two, or even more, before the disease becomes manifest. In some cases the germs would be made ineffective due to the resistive forces latent in the body It is possible to neutralise the effect of these germs through medication. There are certain germs of diseases that cannot be cured by medicines. A fatal disease like AIDS is such an example.

Why does it take a particular period of time for the disease to show itself? It is so because by then the necessary changes in the body would have been completed as is necessary for the illness. In such a period the illness would become fully blown up. The condition of the body would have become so weakened that it would not offer any resistance for the full manifestation of the germ. In the above situation too one could compare the entry of the germ into the body as the commencement of the action or Karma and the full blown situation as full effect or karma Vipaka. I brought forward the example of Karma and the manifestation of the result of that Karma after the lapse of a period of time, as an introduction to this subject. A more detailed explanation of this aspect would follow at a later stage.

When a germ has entered the body, but has not manifested itself yet, could it be assumed that the person would not be afflicted with the disease at some time or other? Certainly its manifestation would occur when the time is ripe of such manifestation. Karma and its results are also seen in somewhat the same manner. From the time of the ;performance of a good or bad deed, to the time that such a deed would yield its subsequent result a period of time would naturally elapse. This is the time factor which is necessary for the ripening of the Karma. It is so because there is such a universal law manifest in nature and Karma follows such a natural law.

By taking into consideration those who continuously perform evil actions but yet seemingly lead a life of happiness, could we come to the conclusion that evil actions would not bear evil results?

When one considers the immensely expansive concept of time manifest in the universe, how could one come to the conclusion that the results of all the evil action performed should bear results in one life time? Could it not be possible for us to think of the long sansaric journey we have traversed, and the positive results that we enjoy as the results of the good actions so performed?

Let us look at the concept of Karma in a very simple manner. The Buddha has explained that Karma is intention or cetana. It is because that apart from an intention there could not be the performance of a Karma or deed. The performance of the deed is associated with the mind, the body and words. It is not my intention here to explain the working of Karma in a scholarly manner. I would like to explain the manifestation of this firm principle in a simple manner as possible. I would request you to re-read the earlier chapter on Mind and cosmic energy. Where does the concept of Karma exist? Is there a place in the universe where all our actions are recorded? Is it an energy that arises in our mind dependent on our actions both mental and verbal? If one were to think on the subject according to the functioning of certain laws manifesting in the universe, the answer to the question would become clear.

Karma becomes manifest through the continuous operation of two fundamental universal laws.

The result depends on the good or bad, meritorious and demeritorious actions that have been so performed.

The results of the actions that are mind-based are termed as Karma Vipaka. I would like to refer to two stanzas that had been preached by the Buddha, to explain the above concept.

> Mano Pubbangama Dhamma mano settha manomaya
> Manasa ce padutthena bhasati va karoti va
> Tatonan dukkha manveti chakkanva vahato padam

Mental natures are the result of what we have thought, are chieftained by our thoughts, are made up of our thoughts. If a man speaks or acts with an evil thought, sorrow follows him (as a consequence) even as the wheel follows the foot of the drawer (ie. the ox which draws the cart).

> Mano Pubbangama Dhamma mano settha manomaya
> Manasa ce pasannena bhasati va karoti va
> Tatonan sukha manveti chayava ana payini

The mental natures are the result of what we have thought, are chieftained by our thoughts are made up of our thoughts, If a man speaks or acts with a pure thought happiness follows him (in consequence) like a shadow that never leaves him.

The two universal concepts of good and bad, happiness and unhappiness have been beautifully explained in these two stanzas.

Demeritorious actions can be compared to the cart-wheel that follows the footsteps of the ox that draws the cart painfully. The results are painful. Expressing it in another way it means that meritorious actions result in happiness, Demeritorious actions bring forth unhappiness. On an earlier occasion it was explained how the mind functions as a chakra or circle. It was shown that when meritorious thoughts enter the mind constantly the chakra gets illuminated, and the reverse happens and the chakra become predominantly darkened with the constant inflow of demeritorious thoughts.

It was also shown that the continuous actions and reactions that take place at cosmic level also manifest themselves in chakras or circles. These fluctuations were termed as dark, bright, black, white, day, night, sweet-smelling, ill-smelling, light, heavy, happiness, unhappiness. When at a time the mind chakra gets illumined and beneficial results become prominent, the cosmic tendencies also react in a similar manner and positive conditions and tendencies begin to function too. These positive tendencies begin to influence the individual. This tendency can be compared to the attraction of magnetism. There is the tendency for brightness to be drawn towards brightness. This condition causes happiness.

This condition is explained as being a state in which happiness is manifest as a result of the good actions of the past. When the minds chakra becomes predominantly dark the results of evil actions become prominent. Negative cosmic forces influence the person at such a time. This is equal to darkness being drawn towards further darkness. The individual experiences distress and pain. This again is a state in which unhappiness is manifest as a result of the evil done in the past.

The individual is a composite unit of the larger cosmic energies of the universe. As such it is not possible for the individual to be disassociated from or live apart from or isolated from the changes or flux of these universal energies. The changes that occur invariably connect up with the individual. The link that connects up the individual to the varying energies that result in light or darkness, good or bad, in my opinion can be termed as the Karmic energy. Consequently due to the manifestation of the varied Karmic energies a person would experience a continuous period of happiness. Or sometimes there would be a continuous period of unhappiness. These can be identified as a period when a person reaps the results of his past good Karma or vice versa. It is at such periods that somewhat continuous unhappiness and trouble manifest both at mental and physical levels. On such occasions one would involuntarily as it were say "There is no end to this Karma. When would we complete this suffering?"

These changes for good and bad occur in accordance to these universal forces. If one were to think deeply as to how these universal forces or energises manifest themselves, it would become clear as to the method of operation of Karma and Karma Vipaka.

If in the universe there is no conceivable growth or conceivable destruction but only a system of continuous change, what law causes the nullification of the result of good or bad actions-Kusala Karma or Akusala Karma? At death or break up of the body, the component parts of water or heat or wind join up with the general elements of water, heat and wind. The hard parts of the body get absorbed into the earth and become part of the earth.

This change is a general universal law that can be accepted. This law can be proved. If such is the general law of things how is it then possible that there seems to be no universal law that influences the break up of the mind of consciousness at death?

What is the reason for the existence of such a different situation? What is it that happens to the mind or consciousness at death?

If when the body breaks up the constituent parts get identified with the wider elemental forces the mind or consciousness at such a time should get associated with a condition that is suitable to it. It should find existence in a re-birth. It should be born again.

If therefore there is no complete annihilation of consciousness as such, could there be annihilation of the conditions that construct and fashion the mind, which really are the results of good and evil action. Such annihilation could not occur. The consciousness of mind that finds re-existence or re-birth will have accrued to itself the results of all the Kusala Karma that had been performed earlier. It will be associated with the so-called individual as a comforting, cooling continuous shadow.

The results that accrue from evil actions are painful. As the ox has to painfully draw the burden along, in such manner unpleasant results follow . The Buddha explicitly expressed these ideas in the first two verses of the Dhammapada quoted earlier. It would thus be seen that the universe is governed by very just laws. There should be no doubt regarding reasonableness and fairness of these laws. These laws are so just, because they determine the extent of the responsibility according to the action. There should not be any doubt regarding the operation of these universal laws. Hence the effectiveness of the workings of the laws should not be doubted by merely looking superficially at the extent of happiness or otherwise that an individual experiencs at a particular point in time.

It is imperative that ones mind must be totally immersed in meritorious thoughts, so that one could continuously progress towards the light. Then the dark film that covers the total consciousness will gradually become less intense, and the mind will get illumined and conditions would so arise that some day it would be possible to end this long sansaric journey. The mind then would be resplendent, pliable and shining. Such would be the Nirvanic mind. Then it would be possible for the aspirant to reach the state of supreme happiness.

CHAPTER V

The manner in which Karma results manifest

Consciousness, re-becoming, merit and de-merit are terms that are intimately connected when one speaks of Karma and Karma Vipaka.

It is the mind or the consciousness that recognises intentions. Conception is commencement of the birth of an individual. This conception or re-birth could occur among humans, Devas, Brahmas, titians or among petas or among depressed states of pisachas or Kumbandas. What is called merit and demerit-Kusal and Akusal really consist of intentions. It becomes easier to understand the meritorious states of mind or consciousness if we were to think of lightness, or brightness and a state of mind when everything as it were becomes non-heavy and is diffused with an aura of brightness. In similar fashion de-meritorious or negative thoughts can be classified as dark, heavy and non-reflective. It would become easier if one were to consider meritorious actions as a luminous power and demeritorious actions as a power that is dark and the opposite of what is luminous and bright. It would be correct to say that in every meritorious action there is an inherent or luminous bright power, and the opposite is true in that which is demeritorious or Akusala Karma.

Conception and birth of an individual occur, according to the results of Karma or Karma Vipaka. It is essential to understand all these so called Karmic thoughts be they good or bad, meritorious or demeritorious that occur in the mind or the consciousness. The results of these various thought processes begin to manifest, not at the moment that such a thought process arises, but after a lapse of time. It is interesting to observe that the Buddha has classified these time periods in which Karma would bear fruit as follows.

1. Karma or action that brings forth its Vipaka or result in this life itself.

2. Karma or action that bears fruit or Vipaka in the following life.

3. The results that manifest in a future existence in Sansara.

4. The Karma that gets dissipated and bears no results.

There have been many instances when action or Karma have borne results in this very life itself and therefore need no amplification. The Karma or action that bears fruit in the following next birth is termed as Upapajja Vediniya Karma. On the demeritorious or akusal side, such bad deeds can be classified as the five heinous crimes. These would be matricide, patricide, the killing of arahats or saints, the shedding of blood of a Buddha and bringing about dissension in the Order of Buddhist monks. To the list of ill deeds that would bring forth immediate results could also be added the acceptance of the view that deeds will result in no fruit, and that there would not be a life after death. Such deeds would have almost immediate results and there strength could not be lessened by any other means. The final result of all these ill deeds, is re-birth in places of great torment, known generally as hells or niraya.

A person who meticulously avoids the performance of the above mentioned heinous crimes need not have any fear in being born in such places of great distress. One can also take courage in the fact that one had been born in a human state in this sansaric journey, and in that long journey even if one had committed the above deeds, then resultant periods in places of torment have now been well passed, because one has acquired a human birth only after the dark period had been over.

Karma has been divided in to four divisions taking into consideration the manner of its operation.

Firstly there is the Karma that conditions re-birth. This is termed Janaka Karma. Secondly there is the Karma that helps and fosters the force of re-birth. This can be literally translated as helpful Karma or in its more scientific term it is called Upathambhaka Karma. Thirdly there is the Karma that generally debilitates or weakens the Karma that has caused the conditions for re-birth. This is termed as Upapidaka Karma. Then finally there is the Karma or force that completely destroys the rebirth Karma and further if a re-birth process has already occurred it tends to extinguish the life process even if it had progressed for some period of time. This force is termed as Upa ghataka Karma.

Let us delve a little further into this aspect of Karma manifestation. The reproductive Karma or Janaka Karma determines re-birth in any form or existence as a Deva as a human, as a Brahma as a Titian, as a spirit as a petha, or even as a pisacha or as an animal. Janaka karma is therefore a force that enables a being to find existence in any of the aforesaid states or places of existence. The helpful Karma or Upatthambaka Karma acts as a helpful or directing force or an inclining force to a being that seeks re-birth in the particular state of its choice. This inclining force manifests both in positive and negative manner. On the meritorious side, the skilful or Kusala thought process generally inclines a being towards illumination and brightness, and hence to a happy re-birth. This force is helpful. It is similar to manure that is put to a plant. It helps its sustenance and growth. The Janaka Karma that conditions rebirth is therefore made stronger by these helpful forces, incline a being seeking existence in the human state to be more fortunate and more noble in his or her dispositions.

If this Janaka Karma or re-birth conditioning Karma, inclines towards a birth in a heavenly state or Deva loka, the helpful Karma would naturally enhance the effulgence and glory of the deva existence. This can be likened to a body of light that is drawn towards further light which would naturally enhance the effulgence. The net result would be the manifold increase of happiness.

How does this force lead on to the negative side. Generally speaking this force increases the degree of unhappiness manifold. If re-birth has taken place in the animal world that existence would be made more painful and more wretched. It can be likened to an animal existence that is to commence in domestic surroundings, but is suddenly prevailed and the occurrence takes place for existence on the way side resulting in creating condition for the existence of a stray animal. Such animals are subjected to much pain and often exist in a half-starved condition. Hence on the negative side too the tendency is to increase manifold the state of unhappiness, that had arisen at birth.

Then there is the action or Karma that diminish the effects of good or bad actions. This variety or Karma is termed in Pali as Upa pidaka Karma. Let us examine some examples both of the positive and negative variety to study how this type of Karma manifests itself. If at the time of conception or rebirth where the tendency is for it to occur into a wealthy family, this process is changed and the birth or conception occurs into a family of ordinary means and wealth. It is interesting to ponder on the part as to what had happened in the above instance. When a positive or Kusala Karma was about to bear fruit in a propitious manner, some demeritorious results arise as it were from the blues and weakens the propitious Karmic result and the conception occurs, accordiugly.

We now come to consider the third division of Karma specified earlier, as that which manifest its results at whatever time in ones sansaric existence. Its importance lies in the fact that its manifestation lies hidden as it were and becomes active when a suitable occasion arise. It is the result of these positive activities that give us comfort and follow us constantly as the shadow. On the negative side the results are painful as much as the burden that the ox has to bear in drawing the cart constantly. This condition can be compared to a spark that lies hidden under the ash. When the ash is removed the sparks burst into flame. This situation can be compared to a germ that had entered the body but stays dormant for some time. When the physical condition weakens, the germ manifests itself and the disease becomes fully established. Such is the result of this Karma in the negative way. On its positive side or Kusala Karma, it is like a seed that had been planted. With moisture and sunshine it springs up and in good time bears tendrils, leaves flowers and fruit.

In this order next comes the Karma that spends or extinguishes itself with time. These can be classified as minor acts of good and evil that is performed in everyday life. It is like a germ that has entered the body but becomes ineffective and its life span ends due to the resistant power of the human being. Or it may be compared to a seed that does not sprout up as its germinating power has been weakened due to seasonal fluctuations and other reasons. Or it can be among a family of ordinary means, preventing the potentiality of a very rewarding rebirth. It is comparable to a film of dirt that covers a lustrous gem. Although the luster is not completely lost, yet temporarily the shining radiance is certainly reduced.

Let us take another example. If as a result of some demeritorious action the Janaka Karma, leads the way for being born as an animal in a wealthy household where though born as a dog, an animal, yet would be able to have a great degree of creature comfort, that may sometimes be even greater than the average comfort, of a human being. This is an example where as a result of akusala Karma or evil action manifesting in creating conditions for an animal existence but at that moment a more beneficial result of a previously performed deed arises and creates conditions for a very comfortable animal life.

Let us take another example to illustrate the operation of the upa ghataka karma. When a rebirth establishing janaka karma is about to come into operation, its potent is destroyed by the upaghataka karma and that particular rebirth is averted and the path paved as it were for establishment of another rebirth consciousness. It is likened to the conception of a child in a mother's womb. But this conception can be made ineffective by a miscarriage or abortion. Another conception can occur but only after the lapse of a certain period of time. Other examples can be quoted to illustrate the operative nature of this karmic result. Due to good Karmic effect a child born to a wealthy family and destined to much comfort and happiness can as a result of sudden untimely death be prevented from enjoying such happiness.

In this instance the child had the essential potentiality for longevity. But this potentiality was short-circuited by the effectiveness of this very destructive Karma. This situation can be compared to a person who had obtained a ninety-nine year lease of a property but by a sudden act of acquisition of the state the property is taken away from him quite unexpected as it were. It would be clear that in all these instances the beneficial effect of good and positive karma were all nullified by the sudden and unexpected manifestation of this evil Karma effect.

The above instances quoted indicate how this destructive Karma goes to annihilate the effects that give positive results. It is interesting to note that there have been even instances where this annihilation has affected, the results of bad Karma as well. It is quite possible for a being whose rebirth has occurred in a place of great distress, to end the duration of suffering and be reborn in a more comfortable setting, Here is the case where the ill effects are shortened and good effects became manifest. This can be compared to the case of a criminal who had been sentenced to a long period of imprisonment, getting a special remission of his sentence due to an amnesty granted by the government in commemoration of a special occasion. Here what has happened is the reduction of the bad effects, because of the sudden frution of a good Karma effect that had lain hidden as it were for a period of time. Taking all these instances into consideration it can be stated that in some instances the good Karma effect is overwhelmed by a more powerful negative Karma, and in other instances the negative Karma effect is completely erased off by a powerful positive Karma effect . We see that conception and birth are due to the effect of the special Janaka Karma. A Janaka Karma that has once manifested, itself, is not repeated or manifested again.

Therefore when once it has manifested, its essential power or energy is completely exhausted.

Karma can also be classified according to its manner or time of manifestation.

First there are those deeds that invariably give results. This is termed as Garuka Karma. Secondly there are those deeds that manifest their results at the moment of death. These deeds are termed as Asanna Karma or proximate Karma. Thirdly there are those deeds whose results become manifest in a priority manner, because of the fact that such deeds have been practised by the being often and continuously and they have become almost second nature to the individual. This variety is termed Achinna Karma. Fourthly there are deeds that had been performed at some time in ones sansaric existence whose results prop us as it were suddenly and become a Janaka Karma, which conditions the conception or rebirth of a being in a particular state or Bhumi. This is called Katatta karma.

The first category or Garuka karma becomes manifest in the almost immediate state of existence. An arahat or saint whose taints or defilements have been completely eliminated attains Nibbana at the death of the physical existence. Those individuals who have attained transcendental states of Dhyana or supernormal states of mind will at death be reborn in the Brahma worlds. On the demeritorious side will be the Anantariya Karma results that had been explained earlier elsewhere.

The second category or Asanna Karma begins to manifest its results when the moment of death approaches. At such a moment, the consciousness of the dying individual turns towards a meritorious or demeritorious deed that he had specially performed. If the thought was meritorious the re-birth would be in a place equivalent to the merit of the thought. Naturally the place would be of light and of happiness. If the thought was demeritorious undoubhtedly rebirth would be in a place of darkness and suffering.

The third variety or Achinna Karma is important because such actions whether good or bad become, as was said earlier, second nature to an individual. An individual who has regularly and constantly practiced and performed positive good deeds, at the moment of death, it is almost certain that thoughts of such deeds would fill his consciousness in the last dying moments. Invariably such an individual at the break of his body at death, would be reborn in a state of happiness or bliss. To a person whose lifestyle has been one of crime and misdeeds his dying and fading moments of consciousness would be filled with such dreadful thoughts and at the break-up of the body at death, there is no doubt he would find existence in darkness and misery.

The fourth variety of Katatta Karma would manifest its results at any time in ones long sansaric existence. Such a thought process would suddenly arise as it were, and become the condition for a conception and rebirth.

What has been explained so far has been a somewhat concise account of the mainfestation of Karma as explained by the Buddha. If one were to seriously ponder on this very deep and profound view of Karma (that had been explained by the Buddha) one would invariably come to the conclusion that as one treads in this immensely long sansaric journey, if one were to cultivate with determination, positive and good qualities of mind and heart, perhaps with the exception of the Panchanantriya Karma or 'five heinous crimes' the effect of all other Karma would with the progress of time be eliminated.

Then the fruits become clear, so that when a person constantly practices meritorious positive deeds, his consciousness becomes illumined. The darkness disappears, The mind becomes less heavy and pliable. Even when on occasions the result of evil proclivities that had been performed by the individual in the past sansaric existences arise, the dark effect of such deeds would be lessened or even eliminated because the result of the constant good would always take precedence.

The example of the life of Thera Angulimala becomes very cogent when one ponders on the object of Karma and Karma Vipaka. He becomes a murderer due to some Karmic aberration that had been done in the past sansaric existence. Yet he had the strength of mind, the latent powers that were there due to the positive deeds that he had performed in Sansara. As his mind was naturally bent towards good, it was possible for him with great effort to develop the latent characteristics, avoiding the evil abberations that had temporarily become prominent at a certain stage in his life.

Finally it became possible for him to completely liberate himself from all defilements and become a perfect person or Arahat, and when this stage was reached, there were no more remaining proclivities that would result in rebirth. What is significant is to ponder on the fact that this great progress from criminality to Arahatship, was made possible during one short life-span. The life story of this noble personage is a guiding light to indicate what super mental heights could be reached in the short period of a life-span. It would thus be possible with determination to proceed on this noble path of ceto-vimukthi or absolute freedom of the mind by the performance of deeds that are conducive to such results which would finally be the realisation of that perfect state of Nibbana. Till this final emancipation occurs, it would be definitely possible, if one were to cultivate positive and good deeds, to avoid the conception and re-birth in miserable states of existence and only be in those happy states till final liberation is won. I would wish to conclude this chapter by quoting the words of the Buddha "Manivatta Abhikkama" - Cease not but progress on the path. Make this your motto and you would never fail.

CHAPTER VI

The dark tissues that lengthen the Sansaric Journey

Once a friend of mine observed rather cynically "Where is the misery of the world you speak of so often. How comforting is it to enjoy a good drink and be quite merry afterwards?" This was his attitude when I tried to explain to him the immense quantum of suffering that we have to undergo during this long sansaric journey.

Another friend of mine remarked, "I would prefer to live long in this world, in spite of all the difficulties, than go after the Nirvana you speak about". The above comments are some of the observations that I received in trying to explain in simple terms the concept of final happiness that is ultimately found in Nirvana. Why do they so lightly dismiss the significance of this long sansaric journey that all of us have to traverse? I think this attitude is due to the fact that all of us are enclosed in a black mist as it were, a dark and intense tissue of greed and ignorance.

It is because we are totally encased in this so called greed and ignorance, that we become subject to an endless procession of problems in this world. From a transcendental point of view, the main obstacle that lies in the path towards Nirvana is ignorance. The manifold problems that we have to face and undergo from birth to death are entirely due to greed and ignorance. Look at any newspaper. The major part of the news report, refers to various dastardly crimes that are so frequent in society. There is no end to reports that deal with murder, rape, plunder, highway robbery and other such dastardly activities.

These heinous crimes have been perpetrated not only by the so called ignorant folk but by both the educated and uneducated class of people alike. The changes that have occurred due to the progress in matters technological have invariably led mankind into a deluge of desires and aspirations. The degree of intensity of desires have been conditioned by greed and ignorance, that have got themselves glued or fixed in the mind or consciousness. What is meant by greed or tanha? This term can be explained as the desire, the insatiable clinging, the strong desire to hold on, to possess. The mind seeks after these desires in the manner of ants that crowd towards a pot of honey.

The mind gets positively attracted towards desires as iron towards a magnet. The individual is unremittingly tied up to the never-ending sansaric cycle by the strong bonds of desire.

Let us consider next as to what is meant by Moha or ignorance. Ignorance can be considered as the strongest of the defilements that influence the mind. All these three traits of the mind viz. Loba, Dosa and Moha contribute much towards the accumulation of kilesas or defilements. Of all these three traits Moha or ignorance plays a dominant part. This has been precisely expressed by the Buddha. If Moha is explained as foolishness or even as ignorance this would be a very narrow intepretation of the word. This word Moha carries a deeper and more profound intepretation. Moha can be explained as a darkness, a darkness that covers and obliterates truth, and obliterates the true nature of things. The term avidya can be used effectively to explain Moha. This Moha has the ability to quickly affect the mind and bring forth a state of confusion. It is stated that Moha is such a powerful defilement, that it would not be possible to eliminate this persistent condition of mind, till the mind is able to reach the noble status of an Arahat or absolutely liberated individual. This state of ignorance prevents the true understanding and comprehension of the four noble truths in Buddhism. It prevents the true understanding of what unsatisfactoriness is. What causes lead to or constitute this unsatisfactoriness. It prevents the elimination of unsatisfactoriness, and the path or method that should be followed for such elimination. It is a condition that prevents the true understanding of the utter emptiness of the fivefold conditions of life. The long and tortuous sansaric life that caries with it immense suffering both body and mental is not correctly realised because of this evil proclivity of mind. This unsatisfactoriness is not physically conceived by the eye, but is only realised by the mind, realised as a mental process.

It may be possible to see a thing physically through the physical eye. Even such a sight would remain somewhat useless if realisation does not arise. This aspect of non-realisation is due to the presence of Moha. It is this evil condition that prevents an individual from correctly realising the immense quantum of suffering that had been undergone from birth to death. It is Moha that causes serious doubts and questioning that often appear in the mind.

Let us for a moment lay aside the consideration of the four noble truths and look into how ignorance or Moha manifests itself, in a normal worldly way. As we have stated earlier the body has five doors or media through which impressions are felt. What happens when such an impression is received by any one of the aforementioned doors or entrances. In such an instance the mind gets activated and immediately recognises the type of feeling, that has so entered. The Buddha has explained such a condition by the terms, feeling, recognition and intention - the Pali term being "Phassa, Vedana Sanna and Sankara and Cetana". When the eye sees a form what really happens is that the image of the object seen falls on the optic centre. When this process occurs, there arises a feeling consequent to the object thus seen. If the experience is mental it can be divided as happy or unhappy. If physical the division would be pleasure or pain. The word "Sanna" or recognition expresses this state of mind. After this process the mind dwells on this particular state which gives way to the concept called "Cetana". This Cetana or intention really becomes Karma action.

All the mental changes described occur at tremendous speed and in the twinkling of an eye, many thousands of thought processes could have occured. These thoughts arise and perish at a tremendous speed.

It would be correct to once again refer to Moha or ignorance as it forms a very vital base for the discussion today. It had been stated earlier that the word "Sanna" can be explained as the recognition of aims or motives. Ignorance or Moha arise at the time of the recognition of such objects or ideas. When a recognition has been made which has been previously conditioned by the five sense doors, does the impression be conditioned or subjective or do we arrive at a correct understanding of things as they really are? In the manner of understanding of such ideas that have often and frequently occurred, impressions are stamped as it were to the mind. The mind evokes a response conditioned by the earlier impressions. This process can be compared to a carpenter who would draw the outline on a piece of wood and shape it according to the outline that had been made earlier.

In the final analysis, could we come to the conclusion that impressions that have been conditioned and subjected to the five sense faculties are correct and formed on the basis of unfailing truth? We come to the conclusion that a form is beautiful and enticing. A beauty queens face is very pleasing. A thought arises according to previous conviction that such a form really conforms to concepts of beauty. But what is the real content of that gorgeous form. It consists of the five-fold material elements, full of the thirty-two varieties of impurities, that are further constantly subject to change and decay. This reality which is the final truth is not seen or appreciated. This non-understanding of the real condition of things as they really are can be termed as Moha or ignorance. Then, if we realise this transition in a somewhat intellectual manner, yet the fact that it does not go deep down to the very base of consciousness the full realisation does not occur due to this persistent Moha. This is an example when ignorance manifests itself through the defilements of Loba or greed.

Ignorance or Moha sometimes manifests itself through the defilement called Dosa or anger. A confrontation may occur with a person who had been earlier labelled as an enemy. Immediately the mind reacts according to the previous convictions. A feeling of anger and distaste occurs. The mind rejects the person as undesirable and vicious. A feeling of detestation occurs. The mind becomes excited and agitated., An element of anger develops. If there had been an earlier conviction that the confronted person is a criminal, a deep resentment develops in the mind. The mind gets enveloped by a dark film or covering. There is a mental darkness as if a light had been extinguished. The mind adopts an attitude of sterness and stiffness. Now your view of that individual is conditioned by your earlier convictions and conclusions and finally decide that he is a real enemy. Your condition of mind could be compared to a person who is born blind. He could never be viewed, other than as a despicable enemy. On the basis of these determinations it may be that a serious and unfortunate confrontation may occur with disastrous results.

It may be quite possible that the person so confronted may not be a real enemy. This false conclusion may have been arrived at due to the tale-bearing activities of another person who may have quite distorted certain circumstances to suit his own purpose.

But now the person appears as an inveterate enemy because of your previous erroneous conclusions. If a confrontation did occur it could be realised what serious consequences would have resulted.

Such a situation arose because of Moha and ignorance. Ignorance conditioned by anger resulted in darkness, and elimination of light and hence the obliteration of the true condition of things. This type of ignorance can occur in the twinkling of an eye as it were and both educated and non-educated beings become subject to its baneful influence.

These three defilements of greed, anger and ignorance can be supressed by the cultivation of meritorious roots of liberality, loving kindness and wisdom. These conditions of mind are diametrically opposed to the conditons of darkness expouned earlier. It is the five-fold obstacles of the mind which are classified as Pancha Nivarana Dhamma that constantly prevent the arising of these positive noble conditions of the mind, and keep the light of knowledge obscured and covered. These five obstacles prevent the growth of positive characteristics, and keep a covering on them as it were. It could be compared to salvinia that covers a clear waterway. When the salvinia is parted, the clear water appears, only to get covered up again when the force of separation of salvinia is removed. This dark layer of salvinia that covers the clear water can be compared to Moha or ignorance that obliterated the light of wisdom.

When an attempt is made to obliterate these evil proclivities of the mind obstacles arise to block the path of progress. The five fold Nivaranas or obstacles automatically appear. When thoughts of liberality appear suppressing miserly attitudes, then the obstacle of craving towards sense pleasures arise strongly and destroys the ideas of liberality.

When thoughts of loving kindness are cultivated, suppressing thoughts of arrogance and displeasure, anger and cruelty arise as an obstacle to the progress of loving kindness.

What attempts at suppressing ignorance are made laziness, restlessness and doubt appear and smother the earlier positive thought process. It would be seen that one obstacle appears each for liberality and loving kindness. But three obstacles namely restlessness, laziness and doubt, together appear as formidable obstacles for the development of wisdom.

The obstacle of laziness is not merely physical laziness, but the state that makes the mind and its attributes non-effective or non-operative. It can be termed as mind inactivity and indecision. This can be compared to a dog that sleeps and thus becomes inactive. This state of mind is so lazy that it accepts each impression or idea that comes into the mind without any inquiry or discrimination or discernment.

The next obstacle is the constant disturbed and un-settled state of the mind. This can be compared to a heap of ash that had been disturbed. It gets diffused and unsettled. The mind is agitated. Such a state acts as an obstacle towards attaining a calm and settled attitude of mind. It is not possible for such a disturbed mind to understand what truth is.

The doubt or uncertainity that constantly appears in the mind acts as a formidable obstacle for the dawn of true wisdom. There is a tremendous doubt and indecision in the mind at such a time. The doubts relate to the Buddha and his teachings. It can be compared to the state of mind of an individual who comes to a cross-road and is uncertain and doubtful as to what turn, what road he is to proceed on.

All these obstacles perform one major function. They obliterate the truth. They prevent the correct realisation of the universal truth that is present. They make it possible for the acceptance of things as are first seen on the surface. They prevent a critical examination, a deep analysis. When questions arise answers are found according to previous decisions that have been made, however erroneous they may be. Wrong views are accepted as truth because of this ignorance or Moha. What is meant by wrong view? To say that ones views are always infallible. He looks at the total universe encompassed in such a narrow view. During the Buddha's time there were six teachers who advocated different views concerning the universe.

A person who does not realise the final truth, but asserts that his point of view is the only truth certainly would go astray. It would be equivalent to the pursuit of a mirage thinking that it is water.

People have got used to ask questions of the type that was quoted at the beginning of this chapter, because of the great degree of Moha or ignorance that envelopes them. There is no salvation from the sansaric strands to those who are engulfed in wrong and irrational views. Such individuals assert that there is no future existence but only the present existence. To them there is nothing called, Karma, and Karma Vipaka. There is no re-birth after death. There is nothing that should be done except live enjoying as long as possible the five fold sense pleasures. The Buddha has identified such thoughts as not only erroneous but definitely vicious and harmful. Those who subscribe to such views would certainly be re-born in very wretched and painful states of existence.

The results of such views would be certainly manifest in the following next birth, as such views fall into the category of heinous crimes or Anantariya Karma.

Ignorance or Moha is reduced by constant meditation. By meditation or Bhavana is meant the cultivation of mind. It is an attempt at "fixing" the mind on a particular topic. It is an attempt to realise the truth of things, and seeing things as they really are, by continuous concentration on a particular object of meditation. When the mind is so cultivated it realises gradually what ignorance really is. Wisdom dawns. There is an effulgence of light. Darkness disappears.

This sansaric journey is a painful one. It can be compared to the suffering of a person on a red-hot iron stake. When this condition is realised intellectually, then at that time the individual would attempt to develop the concept of Vipassana or the ability to see things as they really are-that all component things are impersonal, full of suffering, egoless and empty-Aniccha, Dukka, Anatta. Developing this concept diligently it would be absolutely certain that this individual would cross the ocean of Sansara and reach the final bliss of Nirvana.

CHAPTER VII

The long and fearful Sansaric Journey

An individual who travels in Sansara eventually faces a sequence of events. It is the recurring event of birth, decay and death. This recurring consequence of birth, decay and death occurs every moment, as it were, if the mind is taken into consideration. The explanation as to how the mind changes so rapidly would be most confusing. Hence a simple example of such quick change would be appropriate. Would you consider birth as a source of happiness? Would you consider decay as happiness? Or would death be considered as happiness? If you understand these conditions correctly it would be possible to understand the fearfulness of the long sansaric journey.

When the term birth is taken into consideration, it would mean, through the agency of a Janaka Karma, the conception and birth of a being in a particular state of existence. Such birth would be as a human, an animal, as a Peta or discarnate spirit, as a titian, or as a being in a lower state, or even as a shining one or Deva or as a Brahma in a higher state of existence. Birth could also occur in the four states of misery.

It would be wise to consider the fact that beings who enjoy an immense degree of happiness by being born in the Deva world or the Brahma world, could when at the expiry of the period if its good Karma, and the good Vipaka gets exhausted could be re-born in a lower state of existence and undergo great unhappiness and suffering. This rebirth could be in the animal existence or even as a Peta or departed spirit. Examples of such changes have been expounded by the Buddha.

Let us lay aside all other states of existence and consider the fact whether being born as a human is conducive towards happiness. To be born as a human, firstly, conception should take place in a mother's womb. For ten long months the being is enclosed in a closed womb. Then the deliverance from the womb occurs with much stress and strain. What happens at the moment of birth? The infant cries aloud. Why does the child cry so much. It is not because of a feeling of comfort. It cries because of great discomfort that it had to suffer in the process of being born.

One cannot comprehend this great degree of pain as all persons have completely forgotten this moment of travail and cannot recall it any more. Then the body lies facing upwards constantly. By no means could this posture be termed as comfortable, even if the baby is constantly fed and feels no dire pangs of hunger. But if the baby was born in areas where the worst types of famine occur into a family that can barely meet its financial needs, then its suffering would increase manifold. Think then of the next stage where a child tries to get up and to take the first few steps. Or think of the period of schooling, the period devoted to studies and education. Think of a little child who has had no education but leads its life as a domestic aide or servant. One can imagine the immense quantum of suffering that had to be undergone at every such stage of life.

If one were to study diligently and pass an examination experiencing difficulties of many sorts, then a certain amount of relief would be possible. One tends to think that such a situation would be a happy and consoling one.

One could get married beget children, obtain gainful employment. These can be considered as comforting. But do these constitute true happiness? Or is it the state of not entering into matrimony, having no off-spring, having no profitable employment? Do these conditions constitute happiness or unhappiness? Falling sick, separation from loved ones, coming together with disagreeable personalities, do they constitute happiness? Old age and decay, wrinkling of skin, being disabled, do these confer any degree of unhappiness? Finally would it be considered as happiness, the separation of ones worldly goods that had been so painstakingly brought together, that would inevitably occur with the break up of the body at death. The final separation at death of ones beloved wife and children, would this constitute happiness?

Visit any hospital of your choice. Observe the pangs of great distress that a person who has got himself severely burnt suffers. Observe the immense suffering that is being experienced by those whose limbs have been broken and subjected to severe injury. Think for a moment the suffering and the acute distress and pain that cancer patients undergo.

What happiness or consolation could be there when a person cannot move any part of his or her body and is confined to bed, and then lies in the filth of ones own excrement. What happiness would it be for a person whose faculties of hearing and sight have failed him? What lesson does all this teach us? Is it not that birth, decay and death constitute one mass of sorrow and suffering in the final analysis. Be seated in a quiet corner and ponder on these facts. Try to recall to your mind the various incidents of your life from the time you remember up to the present day. If you were to recall the various incidents of your life, and the type of feeling you had undergone both physically and mentally, would not the list be a very long one? How much of that long list would be considered as pleasant, and how much as unpleasant?

When did a being enter into this long sansaric existence? When did this long journey commence, when did this process of birth, decay, death and then again birth, decay and death, this never ending circle of life and death, when did it ever commence? The Buddha explicitly states that it is not possible to see the beginnings of the sansaric circle. If the Buddha with his transcendental vision was unable to see the beginning of this immense sansara, it only indicates how dreadful and pernicious this sansaric circle must be. Transcendental wisdom means the all-seeing knowledge of the entire cosmos. If the Buddha who was endowed with this all-seeing wisdom was not able to see the commencement of the long sansaric journey, would it not be possible for us at least to comprehend the fact of the immensity of the distance. If we were to take into consideration, the expanse of time into billions of years and aeons, yet there would be no person who could indicate the point at which the sansaric journey commenced.

It was stated earlier that the Buddha with his transcendental wisdom could not find the beginnings or commencement of Sansara. This statement does not indicate that the Buddha was unable to see the commencement of Sansara. It only meant that it could not be seen as there was no beginning as such. This fact can be compared to a circle whose beginning and end could not be indicated. As there is no finiteness or end to the entire cosmic universe, so in the sansaric circle also there is no point at which the commencement took place.

If with the super knowledge and the ability to see the condition of previous lives (Pubbe Nivasanusmurthi Nana) one were to examine whatever extensive a period of time, such examination would indicate that a being had been born, had died and born again, as a spirit or Peta, as a pisacha or Kumbhanda, an animal, as a human, as a Deva or even as a Brahma. This immensely long process of change would be made clear to such a person with the aforesaid super-knowledge. But such a person would never be able to see the point at which such a process commenced. The

Buddha with his all-seeing knowledge, advised us, not to think or contemplate on four unthinkable states in the total cosmos. He said so because there could be no end to such speculation. These four non-speculative topics can be termed as Chitta Vishaya or the subject of consciousness, Loka Vishaya or subject of the universe, Irdhi Vishaya the subject of transcendental powers and Karma Vishaya the subject of the operation of Karma.

In order to understand the above view point it would be appropriate to refer to the story relating to the Brahmin by the name of Upasahallaka who lived in India during the time of the Buddha. Upasahallaka was a very rich brahmin whose status in life was very exalted. He had a large family of sons and grandsons who were equally rich and powerfull. The brahmin Upasahallka had left instructions, that on his demise, his body should be cremated at a spot where other cremations had not been held before. In accordance to his wishes the family members, had selected a spot at which an ancient banyan tree had grown. They cleared the site for the cremation in the belief that as the banyan tree had existed for such a long period of time, there would not be the possibility of anyone being cremated on that spot. They uprooted the tree and levelled the spot of ground and made all preparations for the cremation.

While these preparations were being made the Buddha visited the spot, and was told by the relatives that they were happy to find such an unused place for the cremation of their elder relative and that his last wishes should thus be fulfilled. The Buddha then with his paranormal wisdom saw the actual state of things, and preached to them, that the brahmin, had been previously born into the same clan, had borne the same name and had been cremated at that very spot fourteen thousand times over and over.

This story is significant. If as Upasahallaka the Brahmin had been born 14,000 times over and over again and had been thus cremated, how many more times on this earth he would have been cremated by other names. How many more times in other forms of existence would this particular person would have had his birth and consequent death. Could it ever be possible to estimate or calculate the immeasurable times that this same individual bearing different names and different identification would have been cremated at different spots on this broad earth. It would be impossible to estimate this in terms of millions or billions of years. If as the Buddha stated the Branhmin had been cremated 14,000 times at the same spot how many more thousands of other places would he have been cremated? The quotation from the Pali-Anamataggoyam Bhikkave Sansaro Pubba Koti Napannayati-oh Bhikkus, this ocean of sansara is unending. Its beginning is not discernable. These are the words of the Buddha.

If the sansaric journey is such immensely long and incalculable, on how many occasions have each of us been born in this Sansara Chakra. At the sight of a severely burnt person, lying helplessly on a hospital bed, the thought would naturally come to us "oh, what immense bodily suffering must he be experiencing?" We feel a pang of sympathy and remorse towards that unfortunate individual. Why does not one contemplate on one's own existence. How many times over would each of us have been burnt and would have suffered immense pain in this long journey in Sansara. We are unable to think, wisely, because our minds are covered by a thick mist, through which it becomes difficult to see the truth of things. It is because our minds are enveloped in Moha-ignorance and Tanha-greed that our view lacks clarity.

Is it not wise to contemplate on the fact as to how many times we have on our long sansaric journey would have experienced the torments that are endemic to the four apayas or states of sorrow. If we are able to put aside this dark film that covers our mind and see things as they really are would there be not a sense of fear about this sansaric journey. If the enormity of this great danger is realised even in a minute way then it would be possible to shape our actions in such a fashion that the negative forces be diminished and the positive or meritorious forces be developed.

It is wise to realise this fact because it is one's own actions that condition and determine ones state of happiness or unhappiness.

If the meritorious side of ones life is constantly developed the consummate results of such action would be borne by oneself. Such meritorious deeds would be a good foundation by which at some period of time, it would be possible for a person to be released from the sansaric circle. This strong foundation of Kusal or meritorious deeds will provide a certain positive force that would direct one towards final emancipation. The results of the good deeds would provide a strong inclination towards the goal of Nirvana.

The constant practice of positive, good deeds provide the basis for the elimination of the dark forces that envelope the mind. The hard core of impurities become less rigid, when this happens the mind becomes buoyant and resplendent and shining. Then wisdom dawns as to the reality of things. Realisation then dawns. It is at this point, when the mind is calm and pliable and becomes resplendent that true knowledge or Vipassana dawns. Truth becomes manifest. Then it would be possible for the person to escape from the bonds of Sansara.

Till this final deliverance is reached it is very essential that the positive tendencies in a person be developed constantly. The results of such development would be of immense benefit. The positive results would be manifest like the shadow that constantly accompanies a person. These meritorious actions would confer much benefit here as well as in the hereafter.

CHAPTER VIII

Cosmic travel is regulated by gravity while Thanha or greed activates the Journey In Sansara

The purpose of this article is to assess how scientific the basic tennets of Buddhism are. Experimentation and observation of results lead the way to conclusions-a basic tenet of the modern scientific method. When new scientific discoveries are made former conclusions that had been arrived at are rejected, But it is vital to note that the basic tenets on which Buddhism stands never vary or charge. Its essence remains unchanged as the Buddha has seen through his transcendental knowledge the essential truth that lies in the universe. With this supreme realisation he expounded this unchanging truth to the world at large. The universal truth is Nibbana.

The Buddha expounded universal truths, and not what he imagined to be the truth. The basic tenet of cause and effect or Paticca Samuppada, the law of dependent causation, is the firm foundation on which Buddhism rests. It is interesting to note that with ever new discoveries modern science has to renew and change or completely throw overboard its earlier conclusions. But new scientific discussions enhance the value of the original Buddhist concepts. New scientific discoveries only add lustre to Buddhist concepts. These discoveries enhance the value of Buddhism. This is so because the principles enunciated by the Buddha have a timeless quality . It is cogent at all times. It is Akalika. The supreme truth is timeless. This is so because Buddhism is firmly based on the eternal concepts of Anichha, Dukkha and Anatta-that is impermanence, suffering and ego-less ness.

The correctness of the Buddhist analysis of the world and its laws are enhanced by all new scientific discoveries. This is so because the Buddha did not analyse anything extraneous but clearly analysed universal laws and ultimate truths.

The concept of impermanence and suffering can be termed as the essence of Buddhism. Suffering in its broadest sense is "caused". The teaching of the Buddha clearly expounds the fact that due to ignorance there arises a condition of clinging and hence suffering. There is also the state of impermanence and change which invariably lead the individual to conditions of suffering and sorrow. What is meant by impermanence? Impermanence is change. The transition from one situation to another. The scientific background to the condition of change is the concept of virbration, movement, the state of constant flux. The scientific concept is that a thing does not remain the same even for one moment but is constanty changing.

In trying to explain this universal concept of change let us take a simple example of the solar system in which we exist. The planet earth on which we live rotates on its own axis at a tremendous speed. It has been found that the earth rotates on its own axis at a speed of 1050 miles per hour (mph) Imagine a car that travels at a speed of 70 mph. How would one feel if the speed was raised to 100 mph? There would be nervous trepidation and fear as to what would happen if the vehicle were to collide into another. At such a speed even trees and plants that lie outside cannot be observed. The speed of a vehicle that travels at 1050 mph cannot be easily imagined. It may be compared to the swift flight of an arrow .

It is common knowledge that the earth which rotates at such high speed also revolves around the sun keeping to its own special orbit. This journey around the sun totals to 365 days or it may be 366 days which period would constitute an year. All other planets travel around the sun keeping to their own orbits. All these planets that travel around the sun, together is termed as the solar system or planetary system. This solar system forms a part of the galaxy called the Milky Way which consists of many millions of stars or suns. All these myriads of stars also along with other tiny solar systems travel around the centre of the galaxy. This journey of the stars around the centre of the galaxy takes many millions of years. It is interesting to ponder on the fact that the earth and other planets revolve on their own axis. All these planets then revolve around the sun. The sun and the planets then revolve around the center of the galaxy.

What do all these movements indicate? It indicates the principle of change. It shows very clearly that there is the concept of change that occurs even in such a short period of time as the twinkling of an eyelid. This can be readily termed as a continuous state of flux. Were it not for this vibration, flux or change that constantly occurs, all things would be at a stand still. There would then be no thought process, no animal or no vegetation as such. If there is no virbration everything would become rock hard with only the hard element predominating.

The Buddha was not so much concerned with the physical scientific concept of change . He analysed this fundamental concept of change from the spiritual angle; form the angle how this change affected the sentient being. He related this change to consciousness, to the mind, and related it to the body. In other words the Buddha saw this change, this vibraton, in the concept of impermanence.

The scientific world looks at this process of change as the basis on which many scientific concepts can be built upon. When this change is viewed from the angle of impermanence, it means that a state or condition lasts only a minute fraction of time which is even less than the time taken for the twinkling of an eyelid. In this immensely short period of time, changes that occur in the mind were analysed by the Buddha as a state of uppada, as a state of tithi and the state of banga. In such a minute fraction of time, a thought process is born, it survives and then fades away. This process of change that occurs in the minute fraction of time is a continuing process. The Buddha was able to explain this process of change that occurs in a thought process or Chitta Vithi. Not only the mind, the body too changes according to this law. The cells in our physical body constantly change at a very high speed. They arise, exist for a while and then die off. It is not possible for us to see changes that occur in the mind and in the physical body as there are no parallel bodies with which this change could be compared.

When a space vehicle that had left the earth's atmosphere enters into outer space, the astronauts in the vehicle would not comprehend that they are going at great speed, because they would have no object to compare with what speed they are travelling. Though travelling they would feel as if they were stationery. This same illusion is applicable to the factor of time. We think that there are three periods of time called, past, present and future. In the true sense of the word is there any moment called the present. The present moment quickly becomes the past moment. Is it the person who commenced this article the same at the time the article is completed?

How many myriads of times would the mind have changed from Uppada to Thiti and Banga during this short span of time?

How many thousands of cells that are in the physical body, would have changed during the space of time. This change is characterised in Buddhism as the process of ageing. Why is it that we are unable to comprehend this change. It is because this change occurs at such speed that neither the mind nor the body can understand that the change has occurred. This mental and physical change can be understood in all its ramifications only by a person who has attained transcendental states of mind or Marga-phala. The Buddha explained this change as birth, ageing, and death. It is also the state of Uppada, Thitti, Bhanga, of coming into existence, surviving, and disappearance. This concept of change, of impermanence has not been comprehended by man, and he seeks satisfaction in the completion of bodily comforts. In this process of seeking after pleasure, man tries to grab the whole world to himself. This condition is prevalent because of the great greed or Tanha that assails him to grab every item of comfort possible. All this greed or Tanha is a condition that afflicts the mind. In the physical world too there is this clinging and physics terms this quality as attraction or gravitation. To express this in another way it is the principle of attraction that exists between two objects. This gravitational pull contributes to the particular pattern of behaviour found in the entire cosmos.

If the gravitational pull is annihilated the workings of the cosmos would cease. All celestial objects traverse their particular orbits due to gravitation. This movement would stop if gravitation is eliminated. It is according to this same universal principle, that when greed or Tanha is eliminated, and becomes absent the sansaric journey of an individual would come to a halt.

Sansaric journey too moves in a circular fashion. That is why it has been termed as a Sansara Chakra or Sansaric Circle. The force that compels or activates the Sansaric journey is Tanha.

The physical movement of all things is activated by the force of gravitation, while the force that promotes sansaric journey is Tanha or attachment. In both these examples there is an element of clinging, or coming together,. It is evident how scientific is the aforesaid view point. In the physical world these gravitational forces interact and influence each other. This attracton or gravitation exists in the entire solar system and even beyond. In our galaxy commonly called the Milky Way alone, there are many millions of stars and in the vast expanse of space the force of gravitation exists, although varying according to each of the celestial objects. It is common knowldge among students that gravitation varies according to the heaviness or density and according to distance. This is known as Newton's theory of gravitation. In simple terms when one object gets further and further away from another object, the gravitation attracton diminishes. At whatever distance, a certain degree of the gravitational pull of an object is discernable. This is a purely scientific concept.

The identifying qualities of tanha or attachment is somewhat similar to this concept. A person engaged deeply in the fivefold sense pleasures becomes addicted to pleasures, and can be compared to a gnat that had fallen into a jar of honey. But if one were to distance oneself from such absorbing pleasures its adhering qualities would become less. But by such abstinence the total concept of tanha is not fully eliminated. If this so called attachment is to be completly removed the roots that cause the growth of tanha should be completely uprooted.

These three evil roots have been identified as Loba or attachment, Dosa or anger and Moha, ignorance. In order to eliminate these negative propensities of the mind, a particulary unique system, which can even be termed as revolutionary, will have to be adopted. What sort of change or revolution is this? It can be termed as a complete revolution of the mind. In ordinary language this can be explained as putting a stop to the rumbling of the mind. It can also be called the stilling of the mind. This is where meditation comes in. The mind should be stilled, quietened and made pliable. In this state, through Vipassana Bhavana the final truths could be realised.

The Buddha has stated that the Loka Vishaya is acintaya. He has also said that it is anantha. What do these Pali Terms mean? It displays the immensity of the total universal cosmoligical concept. It is so vast, that its beginning and end cannot be visualised. It cannot be measured in any of the units that are known to man. Does science accept this view point of Acintaya and Anantaya? It was Galileo who first invented a telescope to observe celestial objects. As time advanced scientists have been able to produce more powerful telescopes that had the power to probe deeper into universal space. Newer and astounding discoveries were made about stars and galaxies that had not been discerned earlier, by the use of these powerful telescopes with highly advanced technology. Newer and astonishing discoveries of the galaxy in which our solar system is placed have now been made.

It was around 1990, that scientists at NASA were able to put into orbit the Hubble telescope that could look into deeper areas of universal space. Astounding and astonishing discoveries have now been made and the Hubble telescope has brought to light galaxies and star systems that had never been seen or imagined by any human agency. These lastest discoveries have astounded scientists all the world over.

Before the installation of the Hubble telescope scientists have been able to view through power-ful telescopes star systems placed nearly 10 million light years away. But the Hubble has viewed star system that lie billions of light years away.

What is a light year? A light year consists of the distance light would travel in an year basing on the calculation a number of miles light would travel per second. The nearest star to us Proxima Centauri is 4.3 light years away. Therefore the light from the star Proxima Centauri would take 4.3 light years to fall to the earth. Could we even imagine in our mind what a vast distance would have been encompassed if the star system was placed not millons but billions of light years away "It would truly be mind-boggling" Let us make a calculation and examine the above fact. Light travels at 186,000 miles per second. Therefore 186,000x60x60x24x365x4.3 would result in the figure of

20784286360000 miles. This is the distance in miles to the closest star. Could you ever conceive of the distance in miles of a star system that is placed in the universe a billion light years away?

The Buddha was able to see this enormous immensity of space and time due to his highly developed mental faculty which can be termed as super normal. Present day scientists have been able to gauge these vast distances through the use of developed technology. How was it possible for the Buddha who lived in an age so distant to discover all these salient facts of the universe. It was through his great transcendental knowledge, which is termed as Sarvagnata Nana. It was because of this fact that the Buddha advised the diciple Moggalana not to engage in the exercise of searching for the end of the universe. It is because there is no end. What the Buddha comprehended 2500 years ago with para-normal wisdom modern science has now certified in no unmistakable terms. It is because of this fact that I stated earlier that modern scientific discoveries add lustre to the Buddhist concept of things.

As regards the Sansaric circle, the Buddha made the pronouncement, that there was no conceivable beginning to Sansaric life. The question arises as to why the Buddha was unable to conceive the beginning of Sansara, if he was all knowing and endowed with super normal knowledge. The Buddha was able to see the workings of Sansara by utilising his knowledge regarding the status of the previous birth of an individual. He was able to see the condition of life in previous births with absolute clarity.

Let us imagine that using this superknowledge of seeing the status to previous births, he looked back to 1000th state of existence of the being. This view could extend to over 10000 life spans. He would be able to see all details of the individual, his status, name, occupation etc. If this view is extended to many millions of years or even to aeons, the end would not be seen . What would be seen would be the particular status and other details. As the view extends further and further the sansaric journey is seen but not the journeys end. This is because there is no beginning and there is no end. We have to understand that such a search was laid aside by the Buddha as such an exercise would have been quite futile.

Science too has conceived the notion of an endless expanding universe. Would it be possible to deny the fact in this long sansaric journey each one of us may have been born as animals, many, many times over.

How often would each of us have been born as those of the Peta world, or other such malignant spirits? On how many occasions would each of us have spent long periods of time in places of great distress and pain. Even as a human being do we really lead happy lives? It is necessary to think about these facts diligently and act without delay in order to find an escape from this sansaric existence, which only spells immense suffering of both mind and body. It is very important, very essential to consider wisely the fact in a positive way to escape from all the misery. This is the eternal truth that is manifest in the universe. Working in a contrary fashion towards this universal truth, would make one deluded, and lead to much suffering.

In trying to unravel this long sanaric journey and to discover an illusive beginning, the Buddha looked backwards making use of his paranormal wisdom, which enabled him to see the state of previous existences. His backward inspection was about the long sansaric journey. With such a sight the Buddha was able to see the milepost of this journey very clearly. The clear vision was thus from one state of existence to another, comprising of a very very long procession of existences extending backwards to an immensely long period of time. The manner of existences become clear. But the begining -there was no concievable beginning.

Hence the Buddha took a very pragmatic view of reality. Leaving aside the fruitless search for a non-existent beginning the realisation dawned as to the significance to the cause of things causes led to a result. The result then becomes the cause as well. The Buddha expounded the fundamental truth that a cause led to a result, and if the cause is eliminated then there would be no result.

As stated earlier the Hubble telescope revealed the secret of distant stars and constellations extending over limitless space. If the Hubble is improved upon, then our vision into space would extend further and still futher. But still there would be no end of the universal space. Millions and millions of ever new stars and galaxies would be revealed. This is the endless vision that the Buddha realised through his paranormal wisdom many thousands of years ago.

It is intersting to ponder on the statement made by Professor Cyril Ponnamperuma, where during a learned lecture he said that as science develops further and further the only thing that would remain constant in the world would be Buddhism. I believe he made this statement as he had realised the truth.

As the Universe is "begin-less" and "end-less " what many religious teacher tended to do was to emphasise that the total universe was an act of creation by an all powerful creator God. By doing so they tried to avoid the intricacies that appeared therein. The belief in the act of Creation was an article of faith and hence should not be questioned, was expounded in order to stifle the expression of inquiring minds. But the Buddha opened the door as it were to free thought and free inquiry. He expounded how by clear thought process and meditation the brain cells became more activated leading to superior knowledge. The Buddha was emphatic to show that cells that had remained dormant resulting in a state of morbidity and darkness could be made to function brilliantly by the constant practice of meditation. This unviersal truth was made clear to us by the Buddha. It was also shown how to realise this truth, and to make it a practical proposition. It was made abundantly clear, that each one would have to make the truth a reality to himself. No other agency could provide the truth to us.

It would become very clear that this long sansaric journey, viewed from the point of view of science or philosophy, is fraught with such danger and distress. A being who traverses this immensely long journey would be subjected to much misery and unhappiness. A person who has led a meritorious life and had been skilled in all his actions could find rebirth in a Deva world where he would experience much happiness. After an immensely long period of time when his merit has been quite exhausted, it would be quite possible for such a being to be reborn in a lower sphere and experience unhappiness. This is due to the fact that the effect of positive actions would be over and what would be uppermost of the departing being would be negative thoughts. It is because of this reason that those beings who depart from the Deva world find rebirth in places of misery. Therefore what is most fundamental is to find an end to the sansaric journey. One can never be assured of certain happiness anywhere. It would be quite possible for any individual to be born in a lower state at any time in this long sansaric journey. The Bodhisatta or the future Buddha too had been born many times in the animal kingdom in spite of his great powers or latent positive characteristic. This clearly indicates how dreadful is the long sansaric journey. If one were to realise this fact, he would not waste his precious time trying to see the beginning of an endless sansaric journey, but make every effort to cut short the sansaric existence by the perfection of such activities as are conducive to such a state. It would be fruitful to ponder on this fact for even a few quiet moments per day, as the final effect of such cumulative action would certainly be beneficial for the final deliverance from the Sansaric circle. One must not forget that the great ocean consists of little drops of water. It is for this reason that the Buddha said:

    Appamado Amata padam
    Pamado muchuhno padam
    Appamatta Namiyanti
    Ye pamatta yatha matha

"Vigilance is the abode of eternal life, thoughtlessness is the abode of death. Those who are vigilant (who are given to reflection) do not die. The thoughtless are as if dead already."

CHAPTER IX

Is there a permanent soul that travels in Sansara or Round of re - birth ?

Who is it that travels in Sansara or round of re-birth? Is it an unchanging soul? This is a question that needs very careful consideration. Let us try to analyse this intricate problem in as simple terms as possible. It would be possible to understand the problem if one were to consider the forces that activate the universe. It was stated earlier that the universe is activated on the basis of vibration and the concept of gravitation. It was also somewhat fully discussed how those processes occur. It would be good if this analysis is taken into consideration again. The principle of vibration and gravitation act on each other with a mutual relationship. There are certain natural forces that are manifest in the universe. This power of attraction or gravitation affects the movement of all celestial objects. We have to consider this as a special force or energy that is endemic in the universe. What is manifest here is the constant concept of change. By change is meant the fact that it does not remain the same. It is a constant flux. It is not permanent. In other words it commences, exists for a time being, and then dies off. It really is the concept of Uppada, Tithi and Banga about which we read earlier. Let us visualise as to what happens when lightening occurs. Due to the friction caused by the clash of two cloud layers, light manifests, stays for a while, however short it may be and then disappears. When the light disappears there is darkness again. The process of change that occured here can really be termed as Uppada, Tithi, Banga. This is the concept of constant change that was expounded by the Buddha. This universal change is true of the mind as well as the body. If one were to conceive the fact that two clouds would be subjected to continuous friction for a period of one hour, then it seems as if the light that disappeared in a fraction of time continues for a whole hour. What really happens is a continuous change that occurs at a tremendous speed which gives the illusion of continuity. If a firebrand is moved around at speed, it creates the illusion of a circle of fire. Really there is no circle of fire. The speed of the movement creates such a false impression. This same similar process occurs in the mind as well. The existence of a flame, appearance of the fire brand in flame, occurs because the force of heat consisting of infinitely small particles or atoms issuing constantly and at speed creating the image of the flame. The mind too acts in a similar fashion, and at great speed. A thought process arises, exists and then perishes at tremendous speed. The mind too takes on ideas continuously and in procession. If this continuous change of mind does not take place it would be possible for the mind to be concentrated on a particular topic. In such a state it takes a little time to change from one topic to another. A concept of mindfullness would arise. When such a wholesome mind process is not present, it may sometimes be termed as "blank thought" that often characterises the un-natural quietitude characteristic of a mental patient.

Is there a time gap between this process of change, identified as birth, existence and destruction? If there be a gap what conditions characterise the gap? According to the laws of nature there seems to be no such gap or pause. What really happens is the concept of change that occurs in the same object or the same state. Although there is a constant flux or change there is no permanency. There is no permanent and underlying bond that binds these changes together as it were. There is evidence only the universal law of change.

This change has no physical characteristics. It is only a force. Let us contemplate on the fact that the physical earth is reduced to dust as it were by some force. If all these celestial objects clash with each other and are thus reduced to fine elemental dust, what would remain? What would be seen if a speck of dust is further analysed and separated to atoms, and further to electrons and protons? What would then be seen is a concept of vibration. The characteristic of these waves is constant vibration. This vibration cannot be discerned with the physical eye. Scientists have now come to the conclusion that this concept of vibration is manifest in all forms, physical and chemical.

The electrons, protons, atoms etc that form around this force of vibration is seen as specks of dust and finally as the very globe itself. Why does it become visible in such a manner? This is due to the fact that the vibration inherent in them cause them to adhere to one another. It is the rotation and revolution of the earth that causes all these specks of dust to adhere together in one form as a mass. By mass is meant the collection of matter in a bond of togetherness. If a seed of rice or speck of dust is reduced to its minutest possible unit what would ultimately remain is the concept of waves or virbration. What is done here is to separate the physical elements and to see what remained. What was seen then was the vibrational force which could not be seen as such. The active universe rests on such a force. What does this force do or how does it manifest itself? This force manifests itself in constant change. This change occurs at every moment and is never still.

This constant change that is so manifest in the universe is recognised by different names. It is termed as birth, existence, death, old, age, getting old, getting ripe, getting rotten and other such forms. There is no other change that occurs in the mind other than the changes seen in the universe. This same process of change occurs in the mind as well. The Buddha characterised this universal change as Uppada, Tithi, banga. If this concept is put in other words, it means birth, existence, death or birth, old age and death.

The Buddha used the word Tri Lakshana to explain this universe change. This is the eternal concept of impermanence. Sorrow or unsatisfactoriness and ego-lessness. It is on the basis of this great truth that the Buddha explicitly stated that all Dhammas or things break up and are not permanent. It was also explained that apart from Nirvana and space all other formations break up and last for a short time. Nirvana and space do not change as they are the only two concepts that are unformed. The Buddha explained this change manifest both in the physical and scientific concepts. This change has been expounded fully in the meditational practices dealing with the Tri lakshana concept. Further details can be obtained in the perusal of the Satipattana Sutta. A brief explanation of this sutta would be beneficial.

In the above meditation the classification of a being or person, into Nama, and Rupa or mind and physical form is specified. Nama is the mind or consciousness and Rupa is the physical body. That both the mind and body change at immense speed was explained by the Lord. That the mind and body are constantly and rapidly subjected to this change was explained without an element of doubt. A being that is born to the world is constantly subject to this change from the moment of his birth up to the moment of his demise. He is subjected to this changing process at every moment of his life. It has been stated that the mind changes or a thought process commences, exists and then dies off many thousands of times within a brief moment of time. The body too is subject to this vast process of change. The cells of the body change at a tremendous speed at every moment of life. This change is as fast as lightning.

Although the individual is subject to this vast change of mind and body from the time of his birth, why is it that the realisation or understanding of this change is not appreciated or visualised? It is because of the presence of Moha or ignornance.

This truth of change or constant death is there from birth to death. But a being barely realises this change, intellectually or even casually. Hence he is undisturbed. But when the final break up of the body occurs and consciousness departs, then others get highly agitated and weep and cry at the so called loss. It is this great truth that the Buddha recognised as Tri lakshana. This is the ultimate truth of impermanence, unsatisfactoriness and no-soul -ness.

Would it be considered as happiness, to be born, to grow old to die and then to repeat this process, many times over-would that be happiness? To lose something that one has-would that be happiness? To lose everything one has-would that be happiness? If at some moment of time, one were to experience a feeling of joy and if that were to pass away quickly would that state constitute happiness? When one enjoys some delicious food, and that be snatched away would that be happiness? Therefore change or death becomes invariably sorrowful and unpleasant.

What is meant by the term Anatta or soullessness. If one were to possess something that were to remain the same without any change, that would constitute a permanent self or atman. Hindu philosophy conceives of a very subtle unchanging condition that one possesses as one's soul or atman. If one possesses something that belongs to oneself, that something should remain unchanged. One should then be able to enjoy happiness only without any change of condition. Then it would be possible to remain young always without getting old and infirm, and without ever dying. Even if one were to die due to natural causes, if there be a permanent soul that belongs to oneself then it would be possible for that soul to reappear in a particular state according to one's wishes.

It would be correct to assume that those religious teachers who could not comprehend this continuous process of change that occurs in the total universe become so confused and in order to pacify people adopted this concept of a permanent soul.

The Buddha saw the entire world in the context of this change viz. Impermanence, unsatisfactoriness and no-soulness (Anicca, Dukka, Anatta). The entire essence of Buddhism lies in the above concept. The Buddha expounded the fact that all compounded things in the universe are impermanent, after having fully understood this salient truth through his paranormal wisdom. If everything so compounded in the universe falls in the category of impermanence could there exist a permanent soul, that does not change? If everything in the universe is subject of change, to perish, could there be any such thing that does not change, does not break up and does not perish?

According to the above analysis the mind too changes. It too breaks up. This physical body too breaks up. The earth too would break up and be subjected to change. It would be able to see this break up even on to its elemental form of atoms and protons. Finally its mass could be changed into a mass of dust. If everything in the universe without exception is subject to this vast change would it be possible to conceive of a thing of a so called soul that remains "nitya" or permanent and not subject to any change.

Let us consider the reasons that have been propounded by the Buddha as to why a being travels continuously in this long sansaric journey? This reason is explicitly stated in the concept of patticca samuppada or dependent origination. It says that ignorance condition craving. Then craving conditions clinging. Then clinging causes becoming (bhave) and through the process of becoming is rebirth. Let us now explain this equation in simple terms. Avidya or moha can be explained as ignorance. It can also be termed as a state of confusion. It obliterates or covers up the truth. The ignorance that prevents one from correctly realising the significance of the four noble truths. This ignorance prevents the correct understanding of this, causes the sansaric journey and the results that accrue from it. This ignorance is really moha. This ignorance brings forth a sense of attachment or greed or desire to enjoy the condition called happiness. Of course in the final analysis the above are termed as Kama Tanha, Bhava Tanha and Vibhava Tanha, that is the sensual craving, the craving for existence, and the craving for non-existence. Because of this great craving, this great desire causes clinging or grasping. The clinging to various objects and things, thinking that such clinging would cause happiness. It is because of this great clinging that becoming (bhava) occurs. Becoming can be explained as the conditions manifesting for re-birth. The concept of becoming can be really called the karmic force. It is this karmic force that causes the individual to be born in any specific existence. Again this karmic force can be termed as an energy be cause it is Tanha that motivates the sansaric journey in as much as gravitation impels movement in the universe. This force can be explained as a positive force (kusal) or a negative force (akusal), that determines re-birth. In simple terms it can be compared to the fuel that is pumped into a vehicle, which then spreads to its various parts and conditions the movement of the vehicle.

It is thus seen that desire causes attraction. It is this attraction, that causes becoming -which leads to birth and a new life. This recurring circle finally causes the conditions for birth, decay and death in a continuous and a never ending circle, the cause leading to the result, and result becoming the cause again. It is interesting to note what are the views of those who accept the concept of a permanent and unchanging soul. In the Baghavat Gita there is a verse, the translation of which would read as follows:

"this soul cannot be divided. It cannot be destroyed by time. It cannot be dissolved, nor could it be dried up. This is permanent and is diffused everywhere. It is steady unchanging and it is succinct" This verse certainly brings out the view that the soul is a never changing entity that travels in sansara or the ocean of life.

The Buddha completely rejects the view of a never changing permanent soul. The Buddha understood with clarity the concept of re-becoming or re-birth through his transcendental wisdom. He explained the fact that this re-becoming was caused by the results of the actions both good and bad performed by the individual concerned and as the result of his action or karma vipaka, he is neither the same nor another, "na cha so-na cha anno". The concept of a being who travels in sansara, not being the same, nor another was explained carefully by the Buddha. The re-becoming of a person is conditioned by the last thoughts of the dying individual, and the last thought process is influenced by the persons actions, both good or bad. As long as these prevail in the mind of the individual the roots of evil, come as loba, dosa and moha, there would result a state of confusion and darkness in his mind.

It had been discussed earlier how the movements in the total universe have been conditioned by constant change. All things that exists in the total universe are subject to that concept of change known as Uppada, Titti, Banga. The mind or consciousness too changes accordingly. The body of the individual also changes in such manner. At the death or demise of an individual with the separation of the primary elements the body commences to decay and finally turns to dust. But what of the consciousness of the dying individual. The mind too changes and breaks up rapidly. Then the last thought or consciousness of the dying person, conditions the state of re-birth or re-becoming. It is important to note that it is the last thought that arises in the fast changing consciousness that determines the next existence, whatever that existence may be. This condition of rebirth is thenceforth directly conditioned by the results of good and bad actions performed by a person. This is an ever-changing flux or force and certainly not an unchanging soul.

What is the universal truth that is clearly manifest in the above analysis? It makes one comprehend the fact really there is no person, or "my" and "mine" concept in the final analysis of things. There is nothing permanent or unchanging in the entire universe. Definitely there is no permanent unchanging person who travels in this long sansaric journey. This is the ultimate reality.

Vipassana or Tri Lakshana meditation or Bhavana analyse the body in to the minutest details, and make us observe keenly these various parts and their transient impermanent nature. It makes us look into the unsatisfactoriness of these elemental parts. It makes us realise the total emptiness of things. In other words it makes us realise the total concept of anatta or "no soul-ness". Vipassana also makes us contemplate on the rapidly changing mind or consciousness and to see clearly that the mind too is continually subject to the changing condition of Uppada, Tithi and Banga. It finally makes us realise that both the mind and body are subject to this incessant change.

In as much as the total physical world is reduced to dust, would then be finally seen as a flux of vibrating changing force, in such manner it would be possible to understand through Vipassana meditation, the unsatisfactoriness of the total five fold concept commonly known as a person. It would then be possible to observe mentally this ever changing pitiful mass of impurities that constitute the five fold self or "panchaskanda". To a person with a developed mind Vipassana Meditation can be practiced in the following somewhat simple manner.

It is necessary to consider the fact that the primary elements that constitute the body, apo, thejo, vayo and pathavi; the water element, heat element, wind element and earth element are not entities by themselves but a force of vibrating mass. This is an ever-moving flux. There is no substantiality about these, ever-moving flux. When together it appears as a form or body, when separated there would be no such form. There is only a continuous process of coming in to existence and dying or passing away. This is a ceaseless process. It is thus the fundamental characteristic of vipassana bhavana, to separate the various parts of the so called body, and also to separate the various parts of the mind, and then to observe its impermanence, its unsatisfactoriness and its nothingness (egolessness). Without going into various other details of this Tri Lakshana or Vipassana Bhavana, it would be sufficient for the present to concentrate on the basics which certainly are fundamental. Let us first look at the body and its component parts and realise its essential characteristics of impermanency etc. It would then be easy to see the body as it really is. The body would then appear to be a collection of impurities. Then it would be possible to see clearly the various component parts of the body as if they have been dissected. It would then become manifest that this so-called body consisting of these various parts which can also be termed as impurities, are impure, ugly, impermanent and without an essence. There would then be the clear vision that this so-called body consists of these 32 impure parts viz, hair on the head, hair on the body, nails, teeth, skin, flesh, sinews, bones, marrow, kidneys, heart, liver, diaphragm, spleen, lungs, intestines, mesentery stomach, excrement, brain, bile, phlegm, pus, blood, sweat, fat, tears, skin-grease, spittle, nasal mucus, oil of the joints and urine,. All these thirty two parts fall into the category of the four primary elements that was mentioned earlier.

What is important is to realise the fact that the aforementioned parts have changed through a process of continuous coming into existence, dying and becoming again, this process of change lasting from birth to death., When at the final break up of the body after which the thirty two parts of the body gradually break up and finally perish, to see and understand this process of break up clearly and to recognise its impermanence unsatisfactoriness and egolessness is an integral part of Tri Lakshana Bhavana. By understanding is meant the full realisation, the complete absorption of this fact intellectually. Let us turn our attention to the nama or mental side. By nama is meant the mind or consciousness. It is this conscious state that cannot be realised through the physical senses of sight etc. This aspect has to be viewed from the angle of vedana, sanna, sankara and vinnana. All these are components of the mind. They undergo varied and immensely quick transformation in their own way. Could these aspects which are components of the mind be without change when the mind itself has transformed itself in varied manner? The term vedana means the feeling that the body and mind, experience. These feelings are not permanent. They quickly change from moment to moment. It is this aspect of change that constitutes unhappiness. By sanna is meant the condition by which the mind recognises and previews the particular type of idea that arise in the mind which had been conditioned by the senses eg. the eye, ear etc. This perception too changes and is not permanent. It has to be realised that sanna or perception too is impermanent. The other concomitant of the mind or consciousness which is termed as sankhara or mental formations are also impermanent, subject to change hence unsatisfactory and has no essence. Therefore we see that consciousness, and other mental functions which are inseparable from any consciousness, are all characterised by Anicca, Dukka and Anatta. When considering all these aspects the inevitable conclusion would be that the mind or consciousness is an instrument that change at an immense almost inconceivable speed. If one can fully comprehend the concept of change that the mind is subject to, the concept of its constant arising, of its existence and of its perishing only to arise again in a continuous process of flux then one would have taken a fundamentally forward step towards putting an end to this immensely long sansaric journey. This process of change that takes place in the mind can only be correctly and distinctly understood in its fullest significance by those individuals who have advanced in the Vipassana Meditatonal practices and have reached transcendental knowledge known as "Udayavya Nana" or the knowledge of arising and perishing. The speed at which the mind changes far exceeds the speed of lightning. It is because of the tremendous speed at which the mind changes,. that its significance cannot be clearly comprehended. To those who constantly practice vipassana meditation it would be possible to understand and appreciate the constant threefold change (uppada, thitti, banga) that takes place, clearly.

Let us then consider the significance of Samatha or Tranquillity mediation. In this meditational exercise it is attempted to pacify and "gather the mind together" as it were. If one were to consider the agitated and disturbed state that occurs if a pebble is thrown at a heap of ash, such would be the state of the mind prior to attempting this tranquility meditation. Samatha Bhavana settles the mind of its disturbed and agitated condition. After such quietude is reached attempt is made to look at the mind and see its condition. This certainly is not an easy process. What Samatha Bhavana does is to quieten and settle the mind and make the mind focus on one topic and not allow the mind to wonder aimlessly as it were .

It is when the mind is so settled and pacified that the more significant and far more important Vipasssana Meditation can be effectively attempted. In these Vipassana exercises the entire working of the mind is clearly seen together with the absolute impermanence, unsatisfactoriness and nothingness of all mental phenomena.

In order to reach the above excellent and undisturbed state of mind, the method that is traditionally recommended is the method of "in and out breathing" or ana-pana-sati bhavana. It is an exercise where the natural process of in-breathing and out-breathing is done with awareness. It is through the constant practice of this meditation that the entire workings of the mind and the concomitant factors of the mind are correctly understood. It is encouraging to note that this one single exercise of in and out breathing correctly attempted would result in the complete transformation of the mind from an ordinary worldly being to that of a noble being who has reached the highest holiness or arahatship. It is possible for the mind to reach such excellent heights because as one proceeds in the above meditational practices, gradually the mind becomes bereft of all the evil proclivities, and the roots of Loba, Dosa and Moha become completely eradicated and uprooted so that these evil conditions would not arise again ever.

In simple terms this process can be compared to a physician who correctly understands the disease and prescribes the correct medicine by which the patient is completely cured. If one were to compare the individual who travels in this immense sansaric ocean to a patient, it must be stated that such a patient could not be cured by a physician. In this instance the so called patient must cure himself by strictly adhering to medical advice. But he must himself act accordingly so that his own actions would be conducive to the complete cure. This emancipation cannot be effected by an outside agency, or by a Deva, Brahma, or an all-powerful divinity. The mental cure that leads to final deliverance of mind must be attempted by each individual by himself alone. If you were to attend places of worship from morning till night, or pray constantly for deliverance, such deliverance cannot be obtained by a powerful being living in some part of the universe. This deliverance of each individual from the bonds of misery and sorrow must be attempted by each individual by the constant practice of the methods that had been so clearly enunciated by the Buddha. It is the Buddha's teaching that would finally be the liberation factor that would lead to final deliverance or Ceto Vimukti or the complete emancipation of the mind.

All these meditational exercises have as their aim the obtaining of a clear vision of the workings of the mind and the clear concept of Uppada, Tithi, Banga principle. This really is the understanding concerning, birth, existence and death of all phenomena. In this process the rapid working of the mind is slowed down. This process could be compared to the viewing of a film in "slow motion". In slow motion it would be able to see all movement in such a way as to indicate the process of change. Cricketing umpires use slow motion to check the correctness of their decision. If the workings of the mind is also seen in such a slow process the changes could be appreciated intensely. When this process of changes is appreciated the correct understanding as to the true understanding of the world would arise. Then the conditions that prolonged the sansaric journey viz. Ignorance and illusion would disappear. With the disappearance of darkness there would be a great radiance, and lustre. The path to nirvana could become manifestly clear and journeying along the path would finally lead to complete deliverance.

It would be possible for ordinary worldly beings to reach this consummate state at some date if we they were to persist diligently on meditational practices.

It is of practical importance that these above points be pondered upon constantly. Once such an attempt is made unknowingly as it were one would be engaging in a meditation practice, although it may be in a very elementary manner. Yet for all by constant practice a certain development, a calmness may become manifest. Undoubtedly this meditational practice of in and out breathing constantly and steadily practiced would bring about vast beneficial changes in mind and attitudes. Finally, it is absolutely certain that the path would lead to the realisation of Nibbana, however distant that day may be. A flowing river can never be turned backwards. In such manner the progressive exercise commenced can never be reversed.

It is essential to have confidence and trust in the Buddha's explanations and expositions. Decide to work towards this goal diligently. Then it would be possible for you to lead the life you are leading at present in a much happier and more meaningful manner. It is my intention to conclude this chapter by citing a story which took place during the time of the Buddha.

There was a group of Bhikkus who obtained topics of meditation from the Buddha and returned to the solitude of forest glades in order to meditate and obtain release. In spite of great effort they did not meet with any success and hence decided to visit the Buddha to find out the reason for their failure. When they reported the matter to the Buddha, he was able to use his paranormal wisdom to look into their previous existences and ascertain what topics of meditation would best suit them. The Buddha was able to discern this fact that these very Bhikkus had during the time of Buddha Kasyapa practiced Vipassana Meditation consisting of the concepts of Anicca, Dukkka and Anatta, and hence recommended to them that they should adopt this particular meditational practice. Because of their sansaric inclination they were able to attain final release by Vippassana meditation, in a short period of time.

It would thus be seen that Vipassana Bhavana is very potent and even if practiced in elementary form would bear good results at some time in sansara or other. This would be a good foundation even if deliverance is not obtained at present, to perfect the practice in the dispensation of the future Buddha Maithriya.

"Listen carefully and bear it well in mind".

CHAPTER X

We are one Family In Sansara

There is so much of dissension in the world today. Communal tension is fast spreading. Genocide, or to use a somewhat respectable term, ethnic cleansing, has reached alarming proportions. There is religious tension, racial tension and even caste tension. Humanity has become so degraded and brutality has become the accepted norm. Human considerations have been so degraded that animal nature seems to be more elevated than that of the human. The above indicates the general opinion prevalent among people today. It would be understood that the above distortion of human values has been primarily due to egoist concepts that have been rooted in the human mind. The concept of "I" and "mine" has dominated our thinking in the present day world.

From the religious or philosophical angle this "I" concept or ego concept would condition the thinking process until a person is able to reach the high mental attitude of sotapanna or one who has "entered the stream". But this baneful ego concept has become accentuated in the present day due to the fast progress made in technological studies, which has resulted in creating conditions for the enjoyment of sense pleasures to an almost alarming degree. The background to this persistent and pernicious desire for self aggrandizement is the stubborn concept of ignorance or moha that envelopes beings. This insatiable greed causes tension and conflict in society.

Why is there this conflict? With whom do we have this conflict? Is there any fruitful result emanating from this conflict? Would there be such a conflict if the aims of life are clearly seen and appreciated. I think it would be profitable to consider carefully as to who we are according to Buddhist principles and standards. In order to make this understanding more meaningful let us consider the following facts.

The universe is infinite and has no end. The beginnings of this long sansaric journey is inconceivable. There is nothing in the universe, that is completely destroyed. There is nothing in the universe, that can be called new that had been added to its composition. If this be so, what is it that happens in the total universe? What really happens is the universal fact that all things constantly change in the universe. The elemental physical forces change, and the individual is born dies and is born again, in an unending circle of births and deaths. This is really the concept of birth, existence, death, which in another form can be called Uppada, Tithi and Banga.

My intention in these articles has been to explain the Buddhist concept of truth, and if you had followed the arguments coherently my intention would be very clear to the reader. Let us consider the fact of the boundless expansive universe. Even if it would be possible to estimate the quantum of stars and planets to that of the grains of sand on earth, yet the equation would not be complete. Even the Buddha with his paranormal wisdom did not attempt to see the beginnings of Sansara, as that would be a useless task, how very very difficult would it be for the ordinary normal mind to comprehend this situation? The Buddha in no unmistakable terms expressed the view that there was no beginning to the long Sansaric journey. The reply the Buddha gave to the Brahmin Janussoni was mentioned earlier. It was stated earlier that the Brahmin Upasahallaka had been cremated 14,000 times over and over again at the same spot. This fact would indicate the immensely long Sansaric journey that this Brahmin would have undertaken. One individual who had entered this Sansaric circle would have travelled through long periods of time, incalculably long spanning aeons and aeons being born as sentient beings in different states of existence.

What is meant by this long Sansaric journey? What really is its significance? To put it in words of common usage it means the appearance of a being in places of great suffering, then in the animal kingdom, from there in the world of human from there to the Deva Lokas or heavens, from there to places of great suffering again, back to the animal kingdom then to the human existence, from there to the Deva worlds and next to the higher world of Brahmas back again to the Deva world and from there again to human existence. This signifies the continuous process of births and deaths that occur in an almost never-ending process of continuity. This unending continuous journey would exist until the sentient being attains the final release on the realisation of Nibbana.

It has to be realised that a being finds existence in a particular state strictly according to the results or vipaka of his deeds or karma. This conditioning is caused by the manifold meritorious and demeritorious deeds performed by the individual at different stages of his existence. The seriousness of this statement lies in the fact that as an individual would have performed both good and evil actions, that he himself would have to pay the price as it were for these varied actions. Even if one were to be born as a Deva or a Brahma as the immediate result of good actions, when the resulting period is over and complete, he would be released from such states of happiness, and then find re-birth in less congenial states as the result of the remaining bad karma. It will have to be realised that even if a being would have spent an immensely long period of time in a state of great happiness as relevant to the Deva and Brahma worlds when at some time that long period comes to an end, then the resulting bad vipaka will become uppermost, and the being would depart form the state of happiness, and find existence in places or states of great unhappiness. As in places of happiness in the regions of great suffering too the period of existence would be immensely long. It would thus be seen how dreadful this long Sansaric journey can be.

Think of the fact that if one were to be born in the next life into a clan that one had considered as an enemy previously. Then the so called saviour of the former clan would now be its destroyer. This could be considered as a joke were it not for its very tragic consequences. It is because of ignorance or Moha that blinds us, and that such situations become manifest. If the true condition of things be known would we ever commit such a crime, it is ignorance that covers and prevents true understanding.

The above facts are also cogent in considering the salient fact that we are one family, knit together closely in the long Sansaric journey. Would one be surprised to hear the fact that it is the same life force, of course with particular changes and mutations that appear at different times in Sansara? There is no new or additional forces that come on anew. It is on this assumption that it was said earlier that all belong to one large family in the universal concept of things. When compared to the immense expanse of universal space, the earth's size cannot even be compared to a speck of dust. If the earth is such a minute speck in the total universal space, how insignificant must be the beings who inhabit the earth? The universe is infinite in structure, and time too is infinite. In comparison how small would the whole solar system be when compared to the total cosmic space? Some of these concepts are so vast and baffling that they cannot be encompassed by the ordinary human intelligence.

What is the normal life span of a human being?. Let it be 80 years or a hundred years. Sometimes it could be extended to even 120 years. But the so called human life span, when compared to the life span relevant to the Deva world or the Brahma world would be so short as to be comparable to the twinkling of an eye. It is said that the life span of a Deva in the Tava-tinsa heaven would be over

30 million years. The life span in the Brahma world is measured in terms of kalpas or aeons. The status of a king in the human existence could be compared to the status of a beggar when compared to the great happiness and prosperity relevant to the Deva worlds. In the niraya worlds or hells the life span is calculated in tens of thousands of years. The suffering that has to be endured in the states of unhappiness cannot be expressed in words as much as the great states of happiness and bliss in the Deva worlds could not be explained according to human standards. All this would indicate the fact that when compared to the cosmic concepts of time, the life span in the human existence is infinitely small and little.

The total number of beings living in this infinitely small speck called earth, would also be very small compared to cosmic standards. Although the place of existence may be so small, yet the period of time that a being exists totally in the universe is immensely long. When a limited number of sentient beings die and are re-born many times over to die again and again to be re-born, is it not possible that such individuals may not have had some relationship or kindredship to each other many times over? This relationship is established when beings die and are born again in different families, different, states and different climes so that in the real sense a linking process of relationship is established in a most imperceptible and subtle manner. Would it therefore be possible for any being to reject the fact in the long period of Sansaric existence, that someone else would not have been his mother, father, child or nephew or had some other form of relationship, so established. It would therefore be impossible to recognise that some one else would not have been a relation or had some such close affinity and link to one another. The Buddha explicitly clarified this essential truth at various times making use of his paranormal wisdom.

Why does man who possesses a superior intelligence not realise this significant fact of life? If the fact is realised would there be such vicious killings and slaughter, when the significant underlying fact being that the person massacred and slaughtered are ones own kith and kin? Are they not putting to torture a being that had been our mother or father, or any such other relation at some time in the sansaric existence.

Consider the great massacre of beings that is taking place in distant places in the globe like Ethiopia and Somalia. Think of the famine-stricken, disease-stricken areas of the globe where virtually millions are dying due to lack of water to quench their thirst. Are we not more concerned to conquer the world because of the great thirst for power, political and otherwise, that urge people to produce weapons of great destruction at tremendous costs, while millions and millions of our relatives are dying literally like flies in parched up desolate regions. Many are destined to live lives of great comfort and immense physical satisfaction, while a large mass of beings who really are our kith and kin are experiencing such tremendous and unbelievable suffering. Yet are we not oblivious to the fact that all this mass of suffering has been linked to each one of us at some time or other in the immensely long journey called life? This is a tremendous and explosive fact on which every thinking individual should ponder and concentrate on.

In our own areas of living, how many engage in such nefarious activities as witchcraft, mantrams and spells in order to destroy a so called enemy? How many lay in wait secretly to eliminate an opponent in order to obtain some insignificant political power?

Are we not envious of the success of others and jealous of the benefits that are being enjoyed while we are bereft of such privileges? What an appalling realisation would dawn when it is realised that all these cruel actions are being perpetrated by us on our own kith and kin of a distant past. Why do we not consider the fact that when racial and caste discrimination lead to violence and assassinations, that in some time past we ourselves would have been born into such families and classes against whom we are perpetrating these very crimes now?

It would be most wise to consider the end results that would accrue and follow inevitably the footsteps of such ill doers. According to the Karmic law who would have to pay the price of such evil deeds? When will the results manifest themselves? These are questions that should be considered carefully and with great seriousness. Beings are enveloped in such darkness and ignorance that they give scant attention to these basic moral principles.

There are four very rare and valuable conditons mentioned in Buddhism. The first is the privilege of being born as a human being. The second fact states as to how fortunate it is to be born during an era when the Buddha's dispensation is alive and vibrant. The third fact relates to the condition when a person is able to acquire merit. And the fourth specifies how fortunate it is to be able to hear the Dhamma or Buddha's message.

The second fact relates not only to the period where an enlightened one or Buddha actually lives, but also covers the period of the entire dispensation when the Great One's message is diffused and correctly understood. The Buddha had specifically stated that one who sees or realises the Dhamma sees him as well.

The third condition relates to the places where a being finds existence, when it would be quite possible for him to engage in such activities that lead to the acquisiton of merit or Kusal. There are eight evil places and periods that are considered as unfortunate by the fact that a person born in such a place would have no opportunity at all to engage in such positive actions that would accrue to him beneficial results in Sansara. To be born in human circumstances, or in the Deva worlds or Brahma worlds would certainly be considered as fortunate. The eight unfortunate places are common knowledge to all Buddhists and need not be repeated here.

By good Dhamma is meant the thirty seven topics in the Buddha's dispensation that lead to emancipation and deliverance from the bonds of Sansara. This really means the correct understanding of the four noble truths as specified in Buddhism. The four noble truths naturally lead the way to Nirvana, which is the highest happiness ever possible. It is important to realise the fact that we who are living at present have all the excellent fortunate background for development. Hence it would be most unfortunate if all these excellent opportunities are not made use of due to neglect and laziness. It would be like letting a golden opportunity pass-by, without making full use of that opportunity. This negligence can be compared to a horse that had been taken to the water, but refuses to drink the water that is so freely available/. The horse cannot be forced to drink. It must drink on its own volition.

We would be considered as really blind if with such excellent opportunities available, yet make no attempt to improve the mind. We still follow aims that are certainly not conducive to deliverance. We are still engrossed in darkness. We are confused and follow the mirage thinking it is water. Therefore it is most wise if each individual would spend even a few minutes daily towards the stilling of the mind which would invariably lead us to great bliss and happiness that transcends all human bonds. Then if realisation is not fulfilled in this life itself it would certainly pave the way for the final deliverance in the dispensation of the future Buddha Maitriya.

CAHPTER XI

In the Sansaric Journey, earthly sojourn is a place of rest, a university and also it is a great fair

In the long Sansaric journey, I would consider the earthly sojourn of an individual as the most suitable place for providing himself with the requisites necessary for this journey. It can be considered as a great fair where various necessities could be purchased. It could also be considered as a great university where experience and knowledge could also be obtained. The period of years that a being may spend in an earthly existence when compared to the universal extent of time, may really be reckoned as a very short and brief moment. Let us think of a person who would be engaged on a long railway journey. If on the way at the various halts he would be careless enough not to purchase for himself the necessary food and other needs necessary for the long journey, he would be subject to much discomfort on the way. The traveller would replenish himself at each halt as he proceeds on the journey. This long journey can be easily compared to the long sansaric journey, that an individual would necessarily have to proceed on. It was also stated at the beginning that an individual's earthly existence would be equivalent to the movement of the eye-lids when compared to the enormous life spans that are characteristic of the Deva or Brahma worlds, or even in the pitiful and suffering states of existence.

In the above mentioned higher and blissful states of existence the life span extends to many kalpas or aeons. Just for an example let us consider the life span that is applicable to the Tusita Heaven where the future Buddha Lord Maithriya is. In terms of human consideration, this life span would exceed 5.7 million of years and more. What would be the earthly life span? At least it would be a few years or at the most, and that too very rarely 120 years. The future Buddha Maithriya, exists in the Tusita Heaven as Lord Natha or Protector or according to other tradition as Avalokitesevera Natha. On the long Sansaric journey Lord Natha has acquired the necessary requisites that are most essential for Buddhahood, and thus rests in bliss and meditative contemplation in the supremely excellent Tusita Heaven.

It is important to consider as to why it has been often stated that the human existence is the only place where one could gather all the needs that are essential for the sansaric journey. Is it not possible of a being who travels through other states of existence like the Deva World, or the Brahma, or the formless states, the hellish regions or in the world of the Titans, to gather the requisite essential for the sansaric journey? This question could be answered satisfactorily if we were to ponder as to what are the essential requisites that are so important for this immensely long journey. The requisites are nothing but merit or Kusal. The positive effulgent qualities which are broadly termed as meritorious deeds. It is very important to explain to the fact that it is only in the human existence that is possible to perform deeds that yield merit that bring forth meritorious results. In the other states of existence mentioned earlier, whether they be in the exalted realms or in the very lower and pitiful states, it would be only possible for such beings to accept the merit offered to them by those in the human realm. They of themselves could never react in such a way as to perform deeds of merit on their own volition.

The Deva Worlds are places of great happiness and continuous enjoyment of the senses, though they are of a much refined order than the human world. As such in the midst of such infinite happiness there would arise no opportunity to ponder on the merit or demerit of any type of living. In comparison the happiness enjoyed by an earthly Monarch when compared to that enjoyed by a Deva would be beggarly in description. It would be an almost impossible task to even imagine the type of supreme happiness or ekantha sukha experienced in the Deva World. But the important fact ramains that whatever be the immensity of such happiness, when that period comes to an end, such beings would necessarily have to seek re-birth in the human existence in order to re-gather and re-new great merit that accrues to their credit through altruistic action which is normally called meritorious deeds. If, of course, at the end of their span of life any unspent akusal or demerit appear their birth would necessarily be in the places of hellish suffering. It would be seen that re-birth in the human world is of a very limited nature.

It is said that those who have practiced higher meditational exercises after their span of life in the human state is completed, necessarily would find re-becoming or rebirth in the Brahma worlds. In such states there is an absolute state of quiet equananimity with neither happiness or unhappiness. A being in such a state would enjoy an immensely long period of perfect peace, and tranquillity.

Such a state could be compared to a period of rest and holiday bereft of the cruel vicissitudes of the normal sansaric existence. So even in these extremely exalted states, there are no direct opportunities for the so-called collection or accruing of merit. What really happens is the state of enjoyment, physical or spiritual, of great happiness resultant to the good deeds that had been performed earlier in Sansaric life. It would now be quite obvious that it would be quite impossible to be engaged in meritorious action in places of hell or great unhappiness. In the animal world the state of suffering and unhappiness is both intolerable and immense. This animal state is the extreme of the continuous happiness that is expressed in the higher states described earlier.

The life span on earth is very short when compared to other celestial areas. Yet even in such a short life span, their are many opportunities by which an individual would be able to obtain the necessary requisites that are essential for the future life in such celestial places. It is for that reason that it was stated that human existence could be compared to a trade centre where many varied goods may be obtained. But it must be realised that all these "goods" are not physical objects as such. These goods may be characterised as mental states. There is the state of happiness in the celestial spheres. We too on the earthly state experience a certain type of happiness, both mental and physical, though limited. There is a great degree of suffering or unhappiness in the lower states of existence. This unhappiness or suffering is also very prominently seen even in the earthly existence. In certain Brahma states there is present only the physical state, with the absence of mind or consciousness. This exceptionally high state, can be realised even on earth, if one were to practice mental exercises that lead to "Nir-Vikalpa Samadhi". But it must be fully realised that whatever state of mental or physical happiness, that would be experiences in these higher celestial states, it is only in the human existence that the supreme Nirvana happiness could ever be realised.

In the long Sansaric journey which was likened to a railway journey, it would be possible to halt at a station for a few minutes and fill a bag with such necessities and requisites for the journey. The requirements may be such as suitable or essential for the destination which may be the Deva world or even the Brahma world. It would be possible for a person engaged on such a journey, to make efforts diligently and end the journey so as not to return again. This condition would be analogous to the attainment of arahat ship , when such an individual would no more return to earth. That would be the realisation of Nibbana.

The world was compared to a great trade fair, with many stalls displaying and selling various types of goods. What are these stalls? In some are sold remedies for the ills of humanity, philosophies and religions that offer such panacea for the ills of the world. Some of these remedies so exhibited and sold may grant a certain amount of relief and temporary satisfaction. But there is no real formula or method by which this long journey would be satisfactorily terminated.

How few and far between are those stalls that display and sell the goods that can truly be labelled as supreme truth? How difficult would it be even to enter such rare places? These approach roads would be narrow and tortuous. Of the many millions that inhabit this planet, how many are really concerned with the supreme truth and how many mistakenly follow paths that they believe lead to release and deliverance.

In India during the Buddha era, there were six great philosophers who expounded theories regarding the truth and deliverance. There were also sixty two variations of views of life, both faulty and not so faulty. Today among what a small minority of people are the pristine concepts of Buddhism known? How few are those who really understand the deep concepts of what the Buddha taught? How many are really aware of the supreme truths expounded by this great sage? Even the so called intelligentsia, do they really make an attempt to understand and appreciate the true significance of the Buddha Dhamma, quite apart from their ritualistic concepts that are so common today? How infinitely small would be that number who would stop at that stall and gather such precious goods that would really benefit him on his long Sansaric journey? How infinitely small would be the number who would really make the effort to cross this Sansaric ocean with the intrinsic value of the goods so collected on life's journey?

What was attempted here was to explain how difficult is the task of realising the correct method and selecting the true path that would lead to the successful completion of this fearful Sansaric journey. How few in the whole mass of humanity have been privileged to understand this great truth? The wise traveller on this life journey would immediately realise the shortness of a life span. He would realise the seriousness and treacherous nature of the journey. He would realise that the world is a university which teaches him the treacherous and evil nature of the world. He would make every effort to learn diligently the universal lessons that would be clearly available to him. He would be able to graduate from the so-called university only if we was wise enough to understand the basic problems of life. If one is successful in obtaining the final degree of competence, then really such an individual would have fully realised life's unsatisfactory nature.

The intelligent traveller, as was mentioned earlier would realise the seriousness of the journey that has been undertaken. He would intelligently choose the stalls to which he should pay attention and purchase those goods that are only beneficial to his journey. With discrimination, he would select those of value and reject the unwanted. Every attempt would be made to fill his bag with such goods that are beneficial and of good report.

In the real sense who is this traveller? He is the really intelligent one, the wise one. He looks at the world with great discrimination and wisdom. There is ample evidence here to indicate to him the fearfulness of this Sansaric journey. He contemplates these with discrimination. What is the bag that was indicated in the story quoted? In the real sense the bag is the mind. The unnecessary goods are the demeritorious acts or Akusal that the traveller has unwittingly as it were placed in his travel bag. He should therefore make every attempt to throw them out of the bag as early as possible. He would make every attempt to cleanse the mind-to control the mind. He would make every effort to sit in quiet meditation. By such actions he would like to cleanse the mind of its evil proclivities.

Coming once again to the analogy of the traveller, he would fill his travel bag with the positive meritorious deeds in a diligent manner. As such after his span of life is over, he would be born in the Deva world or the Brahma world or even once again in the human existence but of greater happiness. It is important to appreciate the fact that the ticket or passport to such blissful existence was obtained here, when he was in human existence, and was able to satisfactorily complete deeds of merit. What does the foolish individual do? By the grace of his previously performed good, he gets a fortunate human existence. But from the time of his arrival here in human form, his attempt is to acquire as much wealth by any means. He is unable to discriminate between what is good and bad. He fills his bags with evil goods. His travel bag is overflowing with the goods that lead him to inevitable destruction and misery. Such an individual can be compared to a person that has been born blind with no sight at all. He engages in all forms of debased sense pleasures. The means that he adopts are evil and ugly. His mind is full of greed, anger, ill-will, and jealousy,. He is always intent on revenge and vengeance.

The other type of individual is always conscious of the manner of his actions. He is discriminate and wise. He chooses correctly. He recognises the evil tendencies and lays them aside with wisdom. As such when this life span is over he is able to arrive in the oasis or place of peace and rest . Where does the evil doer arrive after his life span is over? He arrives at a burning desert, the burning states of great unhappiness, in a place so parched as to be bereft even of a drop of water. He arrives in the world of petas or ghostly beings, whose desires remain always unsatisfied. He would even be born among the titans where anger and hate predominate.

In this place of halt which is termed the world, there is the presence of a person who steers the way as it were. There are also labels to indicate the type of goods available at these halts. By following the instructions it would be possible to complete this journey without undue delay or mishap. At times when there is no person to show the way, then each individual would have to use ones own intelligence and thus wisely decide as to what is good and what is bad. Who is this that steers the way and indicates the correct path? He is none other than the Buddha. At times when a Buddha is present in the world, those who come to him are the fortunate ones who have perfected their Paramis or perfections to such a state that they would come in contact with the Buddha himself. When such a meeting occurs, the wise one, sees wisely and engaging himself in true contemplation, realises the final end of Sansara and thus relishes the concept of Nibbana or supreme happiness. The foolish ones even in such a fortunate period, look aside and be unconcerned with such noble truths, and hence achieve no benefits at all.

The message that is available in the world is the Noble Dhamma or Saddharma. This Dhamma explains in detail the various aspects and steps that lead to final deliverace, When a life is fashioned according to these noble principles, Paramis or perfections are completed, that would inevitably lead to purification, of the mind, the cleansing of the mind. Even if the final deliverance is not completed in this life span he has laid an excellent foundation on which he should build later and complete the Sansaric existence.

It is because of these reasons that have been enunciated, that the human existence, was termed as a university. This explanation becomes cogent when it is realised that the ample opportunities that are present in the world provides enough background for the spiritual perfection of an individual. There are ample opportunities in the world that indicate the way to happiness and vice-versa, the way to destruction and misery. Hence the human existence can truly be termed as a university. It is because of the non-realisation, the non-understanding of these two fold ways of good and evil or whatever other name that may be used, that many take the path themselves towards misery.

It had been stated earlier, that in the Deva world the span of life is immensely long. If one so desires he could be able to find re-birth in such a congenial atmosphere as a result of good actions that would bring such results. But what is the happiness that could be enjoyed in the human sphere, where time lapses so quickly as when compared to the Deva world? When the time spent during childhood, and for periods of sleep is discounted what would be the remaining period of time? Would that remaining short period be termed as a period of happiness?

All this clearly indicate the fact of the briefness, the shortness of human life. In the real sense, there would not be even any time for what is termed as the enjoyment of the five sensual pleasures. Therefore it becomes manifestly clear that this shortness of time be correctly understood in its true implications. This understanding would naturally come to a person who has perfected these aspirations in lives past. This fact has been very clearly expressed by the Buddha in the Maha Mangala Sutta. I quote.

>   Patirupa desa vasocha
>   Pubbeta Katha punnata
>   Atta samma panidhica
>   Etan mangala Muttaman

"To live in suitable and congenial surroundings to have completed merit in the past, to be completely straightforward in life, these are the auspicious things".

What I have attempted to explain in this article have been expressed with such lucidity by the Buddha in the above verse.

The suitable and congenial surroundings can be interpreted as periods in which the noble Dhamma becomes diffused. From all these one important point becomes crystal clear. It is that a human existence is the most suitable time to attempt the completion of the long Sansaric journey. It will also have to be realised that the human life span is so immensely brief, that the attempt to end Sansaric existence must be attended to diligently and expenditously.

It is essential to think of the fact as how rare is the period when the noble Dhamma gets diffused. How rare is it to be born as a human in such a wonderful period? If one were to contemplate on the above facts, it would naturally lead to the perfection of such acts as that which would lead towards the cleansing of the mind of its impurities by meditation. If these attempts do not bestow immediate results by way of emancipation, yet it would be absolutely certain that such emancipation would certainly be fulfilled during the dispensation of the future Buddha Maithriya.

CHAPTER XII

Is it possible for an artistically inclined child to be forced into medical studies ?

It would be possible to understand what the truth really is after comprehending the workings of the mind. By understanding the mind is meant the comprehension relating to the workings of the mind. One aspect of meditation or bhavana also deals with the subject of the workings of the so-called mind. This process can be termed as the recognition of the mind or better still the mental states. It would be appropriate to describe certain experiences that I have undergone in order to illustrate the workings of the mind.

Modern psychologists have divided the mind into what may be termed as layers. They classify them as the conscious level and the sub-conscious level. The coarse mind and the refined mind seem to be another classification. I do not subscribe to the theory that there are such divisions or layers of the mind.

As an ardent follower of the Buddha, I am fully conscious of the fact that the final truth or satya can be fully realised by following scrupulously the path indicated by the Buddha. This is so because an enlightened being, states truths and never untruths. By the process of the cultivation of the mind according to the principles laid down by the Buddha it is possible to recognise and understand the true significance of mental conditions and consciousness. The Enlightened Ones have seen this division as mind and mental concomitants - (citta and chaitasika) . This fact can further be explained as mind as seen by modern psychologists. What modern psychologists have done seems to be based on the mistaken concept of the various mental states being labelled as different layers of the mind. The Buddha too used varied terms to describe the mental states that arise in the mind as meritorious thoughts, thoughts characterised by greed, altruistic thoughts, and such other names.

As long as there is the life-force in a individual, mind or chitta or consciousness is present associated with the workings of the heart. The various terms like conciousness etc. are used to describe the workings of the mind when associated with the faculty of sight, hearing, taste and so on. By "Chaitasika" is meant the condition of greed and non-greed and such other concomitants that are simultaneous in the mind. To express this fact in another way would be to say that the impressions taken in by the doorways of eyes, nose, ears tongue are established in the mind or consciousness. The concomitants that immediately arise in the mind due to these impressions are called chaitasikas or mental states. If the mind is compared to a piece of paper, the colour of the paper, its condition of flexibility its tendency to tear off etc. can be compared to the mental states.

Mind or consciousness can be classified as the "bhoomi" or state to which impressions are attracted, and can also be considered as entrances by which impressions are admitted. This condition becomes evident when all sense-doors are closed yet the mind can conjure up mental pictures basing on the previous impressions that had been implanted therein. It would therefore be clear that mind or consciousness is a state. Various mental commitments arise therein. Various impressions are accepted therein.

Both consciousness and mental states change according to impressions taken in by the five fold physical sense doors. Let us examine this state by taking into consideration, the state of anger that would arise at some time or other. This condition of mental roughness arises when certain unpleasant and disagreeable impressions arise. A state of stubbornness arises conditioned by the above mental conditions. there arise a spell of anger. An element of excitement occurs. The mind gets disjointed and becomes disturbed as if a stone is thrown at a heap of ash. The mind gets diffused and conditions of agitation arise. When the mind gets into such a state, the control of the mind gets very difficult. If, of course, the mind has been well trained, the disturbed condition would not arise at once. But in spite of that during such periods of agitation mind's lustre would certainly disappear and a darkness would settle in.

The above stubborn state of mind becomes manifest according to the manner the mind had been previously conditioned by such mental roots both positive or negative (kusal - akusal) Greed anger and ignorance are evil roots. These are negative trends. Non -greed, non-anger and non-ignorance are positive or kusal roots. When the condition of greed and lustful thoughts arise, the above negative roots develop and go deep down in the consciousness. Through these negative roots distressful conditions develop and an attribute of darkness and confusion covers the mind. These states end in great distress and unhappiness. When there are thoughts of anger, jealousy and cruelty, these conditions go to the strengthening of the source or roots of anger. The mind becomes so hard that it could be compared to a rigid iron, from which sparks fly when it is struck. This condition of roughness and rigidness leads to actions of great misery. At such times a dark film covers the mind. There is an element of ignition. Its characteristics are cruelty and non- sympathetic attitudes. It is such states that predominate the mind of criminals. The final result is also suffering. Ignorance acts as a cover to suppress truth. It confuses the mind and prevents the correct understanding of things in their correct perspective. When deeply immersed in the five-fold sense pleasures, darkness or ignorance become more prominent. It is for this reason that ignorance has been characterised as darkness, that which prevents the percolation of light. The final result of the state is suffering. When engaged in these various demeritorious deeds the dark roots of the mind grow deeper and become persistent. These individuals whose greed and lust have grown to unbelievable proportions engage in the endless enjoyment of sense indulgences, and come to great distress finally. Those individuals with deep inclinations of cruelty and anger engage in the performance of heinous crimes. Untruth and slander are almost second nature to them. Envy and jealously are prominent characteristics. As time goes on these evil proclivities get completely engrossed in their mental attitudes. The foolish individual, as he lacks the power of discrimination to sort out what is good and bad, performs such deeds that are demeritorious and negative. The opposite tendency develops in an individual who cultivates concepts of loving kindness, liberality and discriminating wisdom. The mind becomes less and less heavy. There is a buoyant attitude and the mind finally becomes pliable and effulgent. At a moment of anger the above positive characteristics are repressed and darkness conquers the mind. This situation could be compared to the chameleon that changes colour.

The above change when understood correctly means that the state of mind has changed from positive to negative. From good to bad, from light to darkness. Nothing new, or a new thought has not entered the mind as such. What has happened is a simple transformation of the mind. The change occurs according to the impressions that had entered the mind. The background changes according to the impressions that had entered the mind. This is akin to the preparation of the soil according to the needs or suitability of the seed. When a meritorious impression or idea enters the mind, the background becomes stilled and settled and a sense of calmness prevails.

Let us now pay a little attention to the division of mind usually termed as the upper and lower divisions. When various impressions enter the mind a certain degree or part of such impressions settle down in the bottom layer of the mind. Various names as the 'bottom' or 'sub -consciousness' are used though these terms are rather inadequate to express the correct significance of this division. This so -called bottom layer of the mind can be compared to that portion in a glass of drinking water, where the minute residue that is in the water settle down. When the water is disturbed the matter that is settled at the bottom of the glass rises to the surface of the water. The working of the mind is at such tremendous speed that its movements cannot be normally comprehended by the normal concept of sight or understanding. It is important to understand the fact that the residue of all impressions that have entered the mind, impressions both good and bad, positive and negative are deposited at the bottom of the mind. It is this 'deposit' that leads to the fact of remembrance and re-calling to mind of things past.

Let us take a simple example. Some remember their lessons efficiently, although they may have studied but briefly. To some others the opposite is true. They find it very difficult to remember their lessons although they may have studied for quite a length of time. There is a certain degree by which the impressions that enter the mind are being stored therein. This degree is in direct relation to the attempts that had been made by the individual during his long Sansaric journey to fashion his mind or consciousness. It would therefore be seen that in some this ability to recall and remember is more intense and pronounced than in others. In others this ability is rather limited. In such people their minds are filled with unnecessary and unwanted concepts.

In those who have cultivated their minds this positive or plus quality is more pronounced. This experience of awareness cannot be achieved in a short span of time. This concept of mind cultivation should be continued through many many lives. When the mind is so cultivated, the degree of remembrance and recall of past events becomes more pronounced. To one whose attention to mind cultivation had been haphazard the degree of remembrance is certainly less. There is another side that has to be considered.

The bottom layer or the so called sub-consciousness state of mind gets re-arranged as it were in those who have engaged in mind cultivation for a long period of time. In a person who has so systemetically developed positive or meritorious tendencies, the sub-consciousness too would be re-arranged in sympathy with such positive tendencies. To one who has consistently pursued in the performance of evil actions, his sub-consciousness state would be bent always towards the negative and evil tendencies. In the long run, individuals can be classified as those inclined towards, Loba or Dosa or Moha, according to the tendencies that had been ingrained in their minds during the immensely long period of existence in Sansara. In other words the thoughts and inclinations that had been so deposited condition the ultimate characteristics and tendencies of an individual.

It is for this reason that the Buddha recommended topics of meditation to the various monks after taking into consideration their latent tendencies and inclinations that had been cultivated in their previous lives. He was like a clever physician who correctly diagnosed the root of the disease and prescribed suitable remedies to eradicate the root cause and thereby effect a complete cure. If a certain monk found it difficult to make progress on a topic of meditation that had been practiced the Buddha with his paranormal wisdom looked in to the tendencies that had been practiced in previous lives and then so prescribed a suitable topic that would agree with his latent tendencies, that lay hidden. There is the classic example of the 500 bhikkus who made little progress, on the topics of meditation that they had followed; but the Buddha changed the topic after such examination of their previous lives. He was able to see that these same Bhikkus had practiced and progressed to some extent of the topic of "Tri Lakshana" during the dispensation of the Buddha Kassapa. He therefore recommended this same topic which was familiar to them and had been ingrained in their sub-conscious state, so that with little effort they could follow the familiar path and achieve complete release. It is for this reason that I stressed earlier that attempts made for the cultivation of the mind find sympathetic response in the sub- consciousness state, that may find fruition during periods even long after.

This so called re-arrangement of the mind in order to find more space as it were, should be be attempted in a very systematic manner. If more ideas are forced into the mind when there is no space for such ideas, such attempts would be quite useless. In the physical sense goods can be arranged according to the space avaiblable. It could be imagined as to what would happen if more goods are heaped into a limited amount of space. The overcrowding would become unbearable. A balloon cannot be inflated more that the space so available for inflation. If so done it would burst.

In such manner the mind too could accommodate ideas according to the space available. overloading would result in over taxing the mind that would lead to serious distortions .

There is another aspect that has to be considered. Goods should be stored in places that are most suitable for such storage. A chest of drawers suitable for the storing of clothes cannot be used for the storage of paddy or vice-versa. According to the goods so stored the future development can occur either in worldly matters, or in spiritual or other worldly matters. It is essential to understand the latent tendencies that had been cultivated in the past. This understanding is no easy task but it is not an impossible task either. We find that some parents for no obvious reasons, force children to engage in a course of studies that are most unsuitable for them and which are not in sympathy with their latent tendencies. Could a child who has pronounced ability towards the Arts and aesthetic studies ever be a successful physician or doctor? As an example of the maladjustment the case of Aravinda in Martin Wickramasinghe's "Viragaya" can be aptly quoted. When topics of meditation are recommended, it is profitable to take into consideration the latent tendencies that are manifest. This is as far as the spiritual side of development is concerned.

Ideas go deep down into the sub-conscious state according to the intensity of feeling experienced. This stepping down to the inner recesses of the sub-consciousness is in direct proportion to the intensity experienced. A deep impression goes deep down as it were. The impressions gathered in normal study remaining at a level that is not so deep down. It is the impression that has gone deep down, that rise up to the surface at some time or other and cause immense distress. Very painful impressions can sometimes cause serious distortions of mind leading to lunacy. Female children in a family where the mother has been subjected to immense mental and physical anguish by the father, often develop tendencies of hatred and fear toward other males.

May I conclude by stressing the fact that what is attempted by meditation or Bhavana is the gradual elimination of the immense debris that had been collected through the ages past. When this dirt or impurity is removed, the mind becomes resplendent and pure.

CHAPTER XIII

I am my own enemy

Upto this point we have attempted to explain the concept of Karma, Vipassana Meditation, Re-becoming or Re-birth and Samsaric journey. It would be apt for us to engage in a little bit of self analysis. In this analysis what is attempted is to recognize one's own inherent qualities. It can also be called as an attempt of self examination & analysis which would lead to self recognition. But this analysis should be attempted without any self deceit. If the analysis is not attempted in an honest manner, the result would naturally lead to further self confusion.

In your home you may have a photograph of all your family members, taken at some time or other. Try to pay attention to that photograph. It would be best if that photograph includes your wife and children and as many loved ones as possible. Now let us commence our examination. Place the picture in your hands and look at it carefully. On whom in that picture would your gaze first rest on? Let us see what your answer would be. If you were to answer that question faithfully you would invariably reply that your gaze first rested on your own image and after that it would have strayed onto the others. I had read about such an exercise when I was quite small, although I have now completely forgotten when I first came across this idea. It is significant to realize that in spite of the fact that, that picture contained images of your beloved wife children and other dear ones, one's gaze primarily rested on one-self. If you were to say that it was not so, then I am sure you are one who has reached very high mental development, or otherwise you are a very deceitful person. This of course is the fundemantal question that all mankind face today. It is a question of attraction towards one-self. The correct understanding of the problem would certainly be the first significant step taken towards the realization of the truth of Nirvana. The whole question rests on this persistent attitude of 'I & self' It is a certain fact a person's greatest affection rests on one's own self, more than on any other being anywhere else. It is to this condition of mind that the Buddha used the term 'Sakkaya Ditthi' which may be termed as 'personality belief'. Others have defined this condition as self love. It can also be termed as a stubborn belief that there is a permanent unchanging self that moves and travels in various sansaric existences.

Whatever term one may use to explain the above concept it has to be realised that any attachment to 'self' prevents the true path that lead to Nirvana. In other words this 'self' concept acts as a block or an obstacle on their path that leads to liberation. This is a very serious situation which is often not realised. On the ordinary worldly side, it is this 'self or I' concept that leads to the manifold problems that are manifested in ordinary life. It would even be correct to say that this is the root cause of all the problems that arise in the world.

To explain the situation let us take example of the birth of two infant twins. Let us imagine that in the infant stage the mother suckles both twins at her breast. If one little twin is not fully fed at one breast, it would make some effort to jostle the other twin and reach the next nipple in order to satisfy itself of its hunger. This situation is very clear when one observes how little puppies vie with each other to reach a nipple, after pushing the other puppy away.

It is really the concept of 'self' that causes this struggle. Instinctively as it were each one makes an attempt to fill its own bag as it were. Whether it be a human being or any other being, this strong feeling of 'self' can be considered as natural force that is acquired from birth. It is this compelling force of 'self' identification' that persist throughout life unto death and which compels an individual to acquire all the requisites that are necessary for a prolonged existence in Sansara. In ordinary life this concept is manifest at all levels of existence.

Let us pay a little attention to a so-called conversation between two females. "Please say whether this saree looks beautiful. This was brought from England by my husband who is a Doctor. He goes often abroad. My daughter is also a Doctor. My son is studying to be an Engineer." An intelligent person listening to such conversation, would find it difficult to supress a somewhat sarcastic smile. This mother's conversation is so 'self centered' that there cannot be any other thing than 'mine'. To her there seems to be no other person of importance other than that belong to her. If the conversation stops at this limit, not much damage may be done. But let us take another example. Listen to this conversation. "That fellow next door has fixed his fence taking six inches from my side. Let him come this way. I will strike him with this weapon. Sure I will cut his neck without doubt". In both these instances the motivating force for the talk and action is the concept of self. All crimes in society are motivated by the exaggerated concept of self. This is because we have such a persistant identification which lable persons and things as 'my husband, my wife, my son, my daughter, my mother, my father, my car, my property and my land". It would be evident that to a person so born there is nothing so persisting as this concept of 'my and mine and self'. In any place whether be it at home, at school, at office or on the road, or when travelling, be it in a temple or church or at any other place whatsoever, the concept arises when 'self' becomes pre-dominant and persistent.

This persistent concept has been fostered and strongly brought into being by ignorance and greed. 'Avidya and Tanha'. It is because truth or the true conditions of things, the concept of things as they really are, are being clouded and covered by this dark layer of ignorance. The impressions that are taken in through the five senses are falsely termed as enjoyment. These are generally termed as the enjoyment felt by an individual, or by the 'self'. This concept of enjoyment can be compared to a dog who greedily takes hold of a piece of bone and licks it with great relish. It would not even tolerate the presence of another dog while it is licking the meatless, bloodless bone. A person who immensely enjoys the impressions that come to him through the five senses can also be truely compared to the dog who greedily licks the bone, not tolerating the prescence of another dog, would finally come to grief if it tries to gobble the bone through intense greed. In similar fashion the intense desires that arise in the self would ultimately pave the way for great unhappiness.

Let us turn to a very mundane example. Imagine that there is a very great assortment of tasty dishes laid appetisingly on the table. There are a few others also awaiting the meal. One becomes very hungry and then the intention is to fill one's stomach as early as possible and so satisfy one's desire and hunger, in spite of all others. It is when thoughts 'I' and 'mine' arise that one is inclined to collect, to hoard up things for one-self. If there are less thoughts of 'I' and 'mine', the desire for worldly happiness diminishes. In the long run there is little of de-merit or even merit that he would perform. Such a state would be termed as a stand-still of karma formation. The strands that bind him to sansaric existence would get a little loosened. He would then tread on the path that leads to liberation. It is the self-desire that lead to selfishness, to greed, to cruelty and tardiness. It is the self centered desire that pave the way for all the above evil proclivities.

It is this mental condition that views with jealousy, any person who may be superior to oneself. It is this that leads to take revenge. It is this that makes an individual engage in whatever dastard ways in order to get more wealth and opportunity at whatever cost, so that, he could lead a so called enjoyable life. It is this condition that leads to extinguishing the life of another being, if that individual becomes in his opinion a challenge or danger to one's own life. Would it be possible to eradicate this very dangerous 'self-desire'. If complete irradication is not possible could it not be possible to dilute this desire, so that it would become less perinicious. When this diminishing can be achieved ignorance or 'Moha' becomes less and understanding of things as they really are, is cultivated in some form or other.

With the diminishing of 'Moha' or ignorance even by a few degrees, the understanding as to who this 'I' would arise. When considering this fact the realisation would arise, that the so called 'I' or 'self' has come unto being centering round the 'Karmic' effects of previous life. If the actions of a previous life be termed as a germ, that would cause the arising of a mushroom now. The germ that would fall on a suitable soil would cause the arising of the mushroom. It is generally accepted in the Buddhist way of reasoning, that the last thought process of a dying individual conditions the re-birth of an individual. As the germ gives rise to the mushroom, so the germ that brings forth a re-birth is the result of the last thought process, which can be clarified as Karma. The other inevitable aids such as water, heat, atmosphere and the primary elements of 'Apo, Thejo, Vayo and Pattavi' combine around this Karmic force and create the conditions for arising of the fivefold senses of sight, hearing, smell, taste and bodily feelings and conciousness. This self or individual so conceived and born, undergoes a process of continuous change, of birth and death etc. The cells are born and change rapidly to form other cells which in turn change and die to rise again and then to change again. This is a state of continuous change. Mind and consciousness too change continuously and constantly. To put into simple terms the body as well as the mind exist and perish at every moment continually without a break. It is important to realise that all objects that come within the perview of the eye, also change continually. What does that universal fact reveal? It reveals the fact that there is nothing in the world that remain constant and unchanging. There is nothing permanent. Everything change. The so called 'I or self' change constantly and at every moment. The mind or consciousness of the so called self or I also changes every moment. Therefore the wishes and interests also are subject to the process of change. These desires and aspirations change. It is therefore foolish to consider that which is constantly changing and not permanent as fixed, steady and non-changing. If from such a changing situation could one ever expect something permanent and unchanging. To expect such permanancy from non-permanent situation would be very foolish indeed. This deep and significant concept of impermanancy is not understood and realised due to the presence of 'Moha' or ignorance. This ignorance can be compared to a curtain that obliterates the view and shuts out understanding. I can attempt to lift the curtain to a certain degree and indicate to you what really happens behind the curtain. It is not possible for an outside agency to completely remove the curtain. Its complete removal can only be attempted by one-self. This curtain falls again after the reading as one gets engaged in the manifold duties and worldly considerations. When engaged in such common undertakings, understanding and realisation take a back seat as it were.

Now we come to the most fundamental aspect of our talk. How would it be possible for us to lift this curtain even for a short time. This can be done by engaging in 'Vipassana Meditation' even for a short period of time under the guidance of a competent teacher. It would then be possible to tie up the curtain by the cord of awareness. The events of the world should be seen with awareness and attention. When this process of awareness is developed, the cells that had been dormant in the brain for such a long period of time become activated. When this happens correct understanding dawns. The dark recess of the mind gets illuminated. It is interesting to note that of the many millions of brain cells not even half are activated in normal life. The Buddha was able to activate all the manifold cells of His brain. The realisation and enlightenment He achieved when He saw with the mind the true nature of things as they really are I think, was primarily due to the activation of the many myriads of cells in his brain. It is then that a great light dawned.

In order to eliminate this stubborn and persistent concept of 'self' then would be to develop Vipassana Meditation, through which is realised the concept of Impermanence, Suffering and No-self. Anicca, Dukka and Anatta. With the help of a competent teacher it would be possible to progress carefully in the above Meditation practice which would finally lead the aspirant to eliminate the stubborn concept of self or Ego. When this concept of ego or self gets eliminated even little by little, the mind becomes attuned to a certain cosmic force. You will gradually begin to develop a sense of affinity with all the creatures in the universe and practice the concept of Loving-Kindness, compassion. altrustic joy and equananimity to every sentient being. A great degree of patience will be developed. When this state is reached the aspirant would enjoy tremendous bliss and happiness that had never been experienced before.

If you are a person who has not advanced enough to practice the 'Tri-Lakkhana' or 'Vipassana' Meditation, try to think of the conditions manifest in the universe, Think of the fact that the cosmic space is immese and infinite. Think of the infinitness and the un-thinkable nature of the expanding universe. Think of the fact that there is no begining and no end or universal cosmic space. Think of the many millions and myriads of stars and planets that are there in the universe whose numbers are even more than the specks of sand there are on the earth. Think of the immense concept of time that is manifest in the universe. That concept of time which cannot be even reckoned in billions and billions of years. Think of the infinitely small space that one occupy in this vast expanse of time and space. Think of the immensely short period of time that one would spend in human existence. Try to develop a sense of calmness in thinking over these topics.

When such contemplations take place there would invariably be a qualitative change in your personality. You would realise your smallness, when compared with universal largeness. Then your conceit would fade away. No attempt would be made to demean another. You will never try to exploit another and so fill your own bag as it were. It is through the elimination of self and selfish concepts that one could become a truely fair-minded and just person. When egoistic concepts diminish one would freely become a noble person. When further developed with the elimination of the performance of empty ritual and sceptical doubt, one would reach the noble status of a Sotapanna or "Stream Winner". You are now on the threshold of that supreme state of Nirvana. Once this state is reached, the realisation of the remaining three noble states would not be so difficult. Once on the correct path realisation of final goal would not be much of a difficult task.

The words of the Buddha are very cogent in this context:-

"Putta matthi Dhanam matthi, ithi balo vihannati Attahi attano natthi kuto putta kuto dhanam?

"The fool is tormented by thinking 'these sons belong to me. This wealth belongs to me. He himself does not belong to himself. How then can sons be his? How can wealth be his?"

CHAPTER XIV

"Do you love yourself"

What would be the answer that would be given if the question was asked :"Do you love yourself" Someone may say, "Yes, I do love myself, but also I love others. I love my children, my brothers and sisters, also I adore my parents as my own life". Another person may say "No, I love my children more than I love myself". But really apart from the fact of your professing that you care and love so many others, do you in the real sense love and care for your self? After you have read and completed this chapter it would be interesting to pose the question again "Do you love yourself"? The answer would be fascinating.

What should be done if one loves another? That person or object which you love so much be well cared for, must be looked after. It must not be allowed to perish. In the real sense do you really look after the person or thing that you love so much? Let us do a little self examination and experimentation,. Let us imagine that you have a festering sore on your body. In such a situation what would you do? You would naturally visit a doctor and obtain necessary attention for this condition. The pus and festering matter would be removed first and the sore would be made clean by the application of suitable disinfectants and such medication.

After this a suitable dressing would be applied to keep it free from further infection. If the medication applied is not sufficient to arrest the growth of impurities, suitable medication will have to be taken orally in order to hasten the healing process. Now a days there is a variety of antibiotics that would be easily prescribed for such a cure. The results of all these would be the quick elimination of germs and infectious bacteria. By this process it would ensure a rapid cure and a return to normal conditions.

If the wound is of a serious nature and proper care has not been taken at the correct time, conditions may arise that the infection would have spread wide, that in order to save the life of the patient an amputation of a limb may be necessary. If the infection has arisen in a place where amputation may not be possible then even death would occur through such serious infection.

All this refers to physical ailments. But is sufficient attention being paid to bring about a change in the ever persisting diseased condition of the mind. What attention does the average man pay towards curing the ever persistent diseases of the mind? Why is it that it has been said that there is a persistent wound in the recess of the mind. Let us imagine a situation where a particular person would have done some action that can be classified as detrimental to your progress and welfare. What would be your attitude towards that person. You would constantly contemplate on this so called enemy actions and bear constant grudges against that person, and await a suitable opportunity to re-pay him with such actions that would bring disastrous results to him. This is the normal reaction of an individual, and it remains so because of the continuous action of the enemy within him. The enemy that has taken hold of his mind. This enemy is none other than Loba, Dosa and Moha who constantly influence a person to follow the wrong path.

At first there arises the concept of ignorance in the mind, covering the mind with a dark mantle as it were and make discrimination difficult. At this stage the desire for revenge arises and encourages to act in such a way as to inflict a heavy punishment on that person. This can be compared to the support given to a criminal by his close associates. If there is a set back in the mind then thoughts of anger constantly prop up and encourage the mind to become more and more rigid and wild. When the mind is assailed by the three-fold enemy of Loba - Dosa and Moha, the ordinary placid and quiet mind gets completely agitated and invariably lead to conflict and later to destruction.

In such a situation how does the mind that had been toned down by meditational practices re-act. The mind recognises the disturbing process and every attempt is made to dispel them from the mind and automatically build a protective wall around one-self. Then conflict is avoided and calm results.

In an uncultivated mind there is no such discrimination and discernment when thoughts of revenge arise, the so called "enemy" within the mind viz. Loba, Dosa and Moha give full support to the on coming evil thoughts and encourage them to such an extent so that hasty action quickly follows with disastrous results. The detrimental thoughts that come from outside would be controlled and recognised with a little effort. But it becomes very difficult to control the enemy within. The difficulty is enhanced because the enemy within is always disguised as friends and appear in friendly guises. They come in friendly guise and completely destroy the mind.

This situation could be compared to a wound that is exposed to outside infection. The infection increases manifold and bacteria multiplies at great speed. The wound festers and infection spreads rapidly every-where. In like manner when the so called enemy is seen, the mind reacts violently. When a suitable occasion arises every attempt is made to annihilate the so called enemy. This condition can even lead to the commitment of very dastard crimes. This means that at every moment there is a process of self destruction.

Let us imagine a situation where these evil thoughts have been well controlled and in a way, broken the power of ill results. This situation may be compared to a protective cover or bandage that is put on a wound. What has been attempted is the repelling and casting aside and the evil thoughts are prevented from coming in. If it is found difficult to cultivate such thoughts spontaneously it would be necessary to take in some "medicine" that could straighten this process. This so called medicine to the mind is none other than an attempt at meditation on the topics of "Metta" or all embracing loving kindness. When the mind is steadied by the practice of such meditation that spreads compassion and affinity to everyone including to the so called enemy the mind becomes steadied as a "Inda-Kila" or a well planted post that is not swayed here and there because of any extraneous condition. In such a state the mind would become shining and resplendent.

Let us get back to the so called individual who has done some wrong or crime against you. Such person would inevitably reap the results of that bad deed at some time or other. Such is the order of the universal law of Kamma. But why should you be associated with him in sharing that individuals Kamma result or Vipaka. You would be doing exactly that when you attempt to square up with a person by taking revenge for the wrong done to you. Why should you heap this dirt on yourself in this fashion. Forget about revenge. Have kindness and develop metta. Cultivate sympathy towards him. Think of the ill results that he may have to bear in the future, because of the ill deeds performed by him. Have a degree of sympathy towards him. Why become angry with him and become a share-holder to this bad Kamma Vipaka. When this sympathetic consideration is developed positive signals as to the path that leads to Nirvana begin to appear in one's life.

What satisfaction is there for a person who feels that he has taken a full measure of revenge against an enemy. What great benefit do you realise from such a situation. Sometimes it may be that you feel that you are relieved after such revengeful acts. But is it really so? Fulfilment of a revengeful action will never bestow any happiness or mental satisfaction. There would be a growing fear in the mind that some day some similar action would befall him. This too is comparable to the heavy burden that follows the foot-steps of the ox that pulls the cart. This is a constant tormenting thought.

How comforting would it be to rid the mind of these cruel negative thoughts. The darkness that prevail disappear and a lightness becomes manifest. When meritorious thoughts pervade the mind, the consciousness becomes less burdensome. The mind becomes pliable. The bright glowing side develops. With daily practice of meditation this positive side develops. The constant practices in meditation leads to a buoyancy a lightless and fearless attitude of mind. The attitude towards death would change. Death can be met with fortitude. He would realise that revengeful thoughts belong to cowards. When this positive realisation comes the path becomes easier for the attainment of final liberation.

The mind with envy and mind with compassion, these two aspects should be constantly thought about and analysed. Let us look at these two aspects somewhat closely.

Thoughts of anger lead to distress - to unhappiness both in this life and life here-after. The mind becomes agitated fear overtakes the mind there is no consolation at whatever time. One always lives with uncertainty in mind. There is always doubt and fear regarding others. At death such a person would naturally be re-born in a place of distress. The above conditions would befall a person who is full of envy and jealousy.

A person who is able to look with equanimity or the happiness enjoyed by others, and would feel pity towards those who suffer, possess a mind of such beautiful nature, that it could be compared to a fragrant flower. It is this state that should be steadily cultivated.

Constant pursuing of sense pleasures too lead to great unhappiness. In these instances too the mind gets clouded by a dark film and discernment is obliterated, leading to the perpetration of evil deeds that completely distort and arrest the forward march towards liberation. Why should one engage in such activities that bring no good result either to oneself or any other. Such a situation arises due to an uncultivated and underrated mind. The words of the Buddha again become very cogent.

> Yatha agaram ducchannam vutti samati vijjhati
> Evan abhavatam cittam rago samati vijjhati.

"As rain breaks through an ill-thatched house, so passion makes its way into an unreflecting mind".

> Yatha agram succhnnam vutti na samati vijjhati
> Evan subhavitam cittam rago na samati vijjhati"

As rain does not break through a well thatched house so passion does not make its way into a reflecting mind"

CHAPTER XV

The Newtonial Principles which the Buddha explained 2500 years ago

Let us make a few observations. Do you experience an immense sense of satisfaction when you gain something? When success and fame accompany you do you experience an almost limitless joy and buoyancy. Are you elated, and feel proud when praise is showered on you? When enveloped in happiness do you try to enjoy that happiness in a limitless manner. If you have these qualities you are a person who would become distorted in mind at the least possible occasion when minor mis-adjustments occur. You would be assailed with sadness. You would become quite unbalanced in your attitudes.

What are the reasons for such conclusions. All the above states are experienced in the mind or commonly speaking mentally. It is the concept of self or a degree of egoism that is at the background of such feelings. All these feelings are based on the concept of self and ego and the basic background to all this is greed or "tanha". This can be termed as desires and attachment. The attachment that is persistent towards the five-fold sense impressions. The great unending wish and desire to enjoy all the so called comforts of life.

A mind that is used to become elated diffuse happiness, when success and praise are present, become deflated as it were and become extremely sad when the opposite conditions manifest themselves. In such a mind the intensity of happiness is great. In the same proportion the intensity of unhappiness also become great when the opposite conditions are experienced. What can be recognised as the opposite conditions. For gain there is the loss. For fame and name there is dishonour. For happiness there is suffering and unhappiness. To the extent that a person feels elated when positive conditions of gain and happiness present themselves, to that same extent unhappiness and discontent become evident when the opposite conditions come into play. How do these opposite conditions arise. What are the laws that are at the background of these states. The intimate relationship that exist on the physical side was explained by Sir Issac Newton (1642-1729 AD). He explained a mathematical formula which specified that "action and re-action are always equal and opposite". It is interesting to note that this very significant principle was expounded by the Buddha in relation to mental conditions nearly 2500 years ago, and thousand years or so later scientists found affinity with this concept in relation to physical matters. In simple terms this law says that if the force of some matter extends up to a particular point, its opposite force too extends exactly in proportion to that force in the opposite direction. Let us take one example and examine this statement.

A swing that had been pushed forward recoils back at the same speed. A Tennis ball played against a wall re-bounces back at the same speed with which it had been hit earlier. Science has amply proved this physical law. In any action there is a duality that is manifest. Nothing happens against this duality. This concept of duality is manifest everywhere and in every conceivable thing. There is the concept of Day and Night. There is the black and the white. There is the tall and the short, there is the sweet smell and the evil smell, there is loss and gain, there is fame and ill-fame, there is praise and condemnation. There is comfort and discomfort. There is merit and demerit and manifold such dualities. These two opposite forces always manifest themselves everywhere in the world. The continuous existence of the world is directly dependent on the concept of duality.

The Buddha saw the concept as the eight-fold vicissitudes of life. The term that was used is "Ashta Loka Dhamma". When the mind gets used to enjoy the positive aspect of this Dharma, to that extent the negative aspect of Dhamma also expand. When there is a pleasant and satisfying feeling of happiness, the desire to continuously have this feeling increases. Here what increases proportionately is the negative feeling of greed or tanha. The desire to possess more and more of the happiness increase. This can be compared to the fact that height of a mountain is proportionate to the depth of its valley. So in relation to this if a person who climbs a tall mountain, slips and falls back the fall would be as immense as the height of the mountain. It would thus be seen that the great degree of happiness that had been enjoyed disappear and the distress caused the longing for the lost happiness is intense. This degree of suffering being proportionate to the degree of pleasure is truly a scientific concept, and is pertinent to mental states as well.

It would be interesting to ponder on the fact of a certain incident that occurred during the Foot-Ball World Cup series. When Argentina was defeated Captain Maradona, along with his team mates wept openly in front of the whole world as it were. What was the reason for such display. Why was it so difficult for them to accept the fact of defeat. Their dejection was proportionate to the degree of happiness they felt at victory. Even among World Champions when things of the mind are concerned, they become very much like little children who find it difficult to cultivate a state of equanimity. It is this mental state that makes a player jump into the air with boundless joy and hang on to another, whenever a goal has been scored. All these are manifestations of the great desire that pervade their minds at becoming world champions. They become conscious of the money that they would win, the fame they would enjoy. As the desires expand expectations too expand. When the expectations are blown sky high, their grief knows no limit and their tears are exhibited to the whole world.

What is the remedy that had been prescribed in Buddhism. It is to develop the state of being unruffled in whatever circumstances, either in happiness or in sorrow. It is to adopt a semblance of equanimity and not to be elated or depressed under whatever circumstances. If this mental poise is cultivated it would be possible for a person to face whatever circumstances with dignity and poise, and with undue exhibition of elation or otherwise. If it is truly realised that there is no such person called "I or mine" then such a person could not be subjected to such pain and anguish. The mind would then accept the fact the concepts of gain, fame or loss are only conditions of the mind that have been adopted falsely, which result in all the suffering. Once the truth of "No self" is understood even the true state of things as they really are bereft briefly of the veils of maya or delusion would disappear and truth would become absolutely clear. In all matters and in all considerations the middle path, that avoids the extremes should always be adopted. Then only can we truly tread the path to final victory over the senses. The degree of satisfaction that is derived according to the normal vicissitudes of life, can be characterised as somewhat coarse and un-refined. The satisfaction that is derived by the performance of meritorious deeds, and the resultant thought are sublime and fine and its texture is refined.

The satisfaction derived from worldly vicissitudes are characterised by greed and tanha. The basis of such enjoyment is a concept of the desire to possess. The meritorious thoughts are characterised by the concept of giving up , of leaving aside by a sense of non-clinging. Then the burdens that had weighted the mind get reduced. It is as if a heavy burden had been put aside. These positive thoughts bring about an illumination of the mind. The mind feels eased and comforted. It is as if a light has dawned and the dark recesses of the mind have become illuminated.

When meritorious and positive thoughts find predominance, the evil proclivities that had reigned so far become less and less intense. It would then be possible to reduce gradually the worldly desires that had so tormented the mind. With the gradual development of these positive tendencies, mind's illumination would grow and expand. The correct and true concept of things as they really are - would become more and more clear. Then the doors to Nibbana would surely be opened.

The mind can be brought to such a state by constant practice and attention. This state can be realised by the constant cultivation of the mind. The mind then would reach a certain degree of maturity. The mind would become more collected and stilled. The mind would become less and less impure. It would become shining and resplendent. It is therefore very necessary to devote even a short period daily towards the cultivation of the mind. When this quietening is practiced diligently and continuously a degree of equanimity would be achieved. Then whatever storms that may strike from all four directions would be unable to disturb the quietitude that had been achieved. One would become like an 'Indakeela' or well fixed state, that is not buffeted by the winds that blow against it. Then it would be possible to maintain a poise and calm in the midst of the eightfold vicissitudes of life with courage and understanding. Then the brief life span could be completed with happiness and bliss, and equanimity.

CHAPTER XVI

Committing suicide is like drinking molten liquid to quench one's thirst

Why are suicides attempted? Most often the answer would be that such a deed was attempted due to the inability to bear pain. The pain may be termed as physical pain. It is so because the individual, the self or the ego is unable to bear the physical pain. But it must be realised that there is no being in the wide world who has not experienced some form of pain or other. Even animals undergo physical pain and discomfort. It is only the human species that commit suicide not being able to bear whatever pain that may have arisen. There have never been any instances where an animal had ended its life in such manner. When man who is supposed to have such advanced faculties commit suicide, an animal whose faculties are least developed make a heroic effort to preserve life and to exist. Whatever pain and discomfort an animal would experience yet it would make every effort to preserve its life up to the last moment.

Pain is of two varieties. There is the physical variety about which one is quite familiar. The other is the mental pain or agony that one experiences. Physical pain is often caused by disease and by such bodily affliction caused by an accident or such mis-hap. If for instance the whole body has suffered severe burns, the suffering could be immense. Cancers and incurable and malignant ulcers could also cause great physical pain and discomfort. Although the cause for such pain has the body as the base, yet the pain is experienced by the mind. The other variety of pain is directly by caused by the vagaries of the eightfold vicissitudes of life that bring disappointment and mental torture in its wake. Many people end their lives as all their hopes have been extinguished. If one experiences a tremendous loss, which cannot be tolerated, then suicide is attempted as a way of relief. There are many instances of attempted suicide due to the break up and disappointment experienced by lovers. Some commit suicide when an illegitimate child is born, as a means of covering up the so called shame as it were. There are also instances of suicide due to the inability to pay back bank loans, and also being unable to face socially due to a dastard crime committed. There have been instances due to sudden rise of anger. If one were to think deeply the underlying cause for such a crime there has always been the ego concept or the consciousness of "Self" or "I" or "Mine".

To put this in another way, such person would have said, "I cannot bear this pain - I cannot face the situation". To the extent that the greed or desire to experience comfort has grown to that extent would also be the disappointment on the realisation of the inability to enjoy that earlier happiness. The disappointment would be so acute, and hence such desperate action becomes manifest.

Why do lovers often commit suicide when disappointed in love. What is this so called love that prevail among two young persons. Is it the supremely beautiful attitude of selfless state of mind that pervades all others, and encompass an element of charity and compassion. This love is so divine. It is a very positive state of mind. It is the love about which Lord Jesus spoke when he advised people to show compassion to one's neighbour. This divine consideration is meritorious in concept. This love is mixed with compassion and consideration for others, and also with equanimity. It is with this state of mind that the so called lovers experience their affection. What most lovers are afflicted with is greed, mixed with lust for the physical enjoyment of sensual pleasures These though they say is love are really lustful thoughts of a low order. They are bound together with greed and selfish motives. In its free nature could love and compassion ever lead to suicide. Could such a love make possible a person to stab another in many places, because the so-called love has been denied and given to another. It is not love but pure lust and physical attraction that makes the ego take a very prominent place so that all other considerations and discernments disappear. It is this false considerations of so called love that lead to so much of disharmony and pain. Lust and physical attraction has been disguised to appear as love and with this the idea of "I" and "mine" has grown to wide dimensions.

Discussing this aspect a little further one could come to the conclusion that what had been concluded as love is nothing short of greed and lustful desires in the guise of love. These feelings are crude and not refined. They are impure and ignoble. What has been attempted here is not the display of true love and affection, but the attempt made to satisfy ones lower instincts by the imposition of another image in ones mind. This image is made use of over and over again whenever desire arises in the mind. The satisfaction derived from such an exercise could be truly compared to the action of a dog that greedily gnaws upon a dry bone with great relish. It could be imagined as to what would arise if an attempt is made by another dog to snatch and take away the bone to itself. It is an occasion similar to the above, when situations arise when dissapointed lovers commit suicide and on other occasions with a great degree of jealousy inflict injury on the other that has snatched away the so called "bone of contention". In proportion to the degree of greed displayed, to that extent would also be the desperate thoughts that would assail the mind. To such a disappointed lover's mind, would continually flow thoughts of desperation and evil inclination. These thoughts would flow at such speed that it would be almost impossible to escape from their pernicious influence. This condition could be compared to a truly burning sensation that arise from the lower regions and work up literally towards the heart as well. These tormenting thoughts are so intense, that whatever task the person would try to engage himself, these tormenting evil considerations would overwhelm him at all times. The mind would be constantly tormented by the thought of the loss sustained, and become extremely jealous of the person who has been able to win his erstwhile object of affection. The mind would be completely disturbed and lose its sense of balance. It would get agitated. Thoughts of revenge would be uppermost in the mind. His mealtime would be so disturbed that no food could really be digested. He would put aside his meals. He would enjoy no sleep attempt any duties that would be his due share. The mind would be in a constant state of agitation. At office he would not find enough concentration to attempt any duties that would be his due share. He would roll from side to side in his bed unable to get even a snatch of sleep. The work would get into arrears. He would be enmeshed in a net of disturbing thoughts ideas and imaginary fears. At this stage comfort would be sought in burning away endless cigarettes. He would seek solace in intoxicating drinks. When the drugged effect of liquor pass off, he would again commence to brood on the losses he had incurred. Enmeshed in these desperate thoughts he would become so helpless and forlorn. At this stage he would even think of killing and putting an end to the life of his enemy. If that aim cannot be achieved he would become more forlorn and more desperate. He would become a total failure, a total wreck.

There is no escape from this dire situation now. He would then desperately consider himself as a total failure to whom there would never be a way of escape from the mental tortures that is his lot to endure. He is desolate and alone with no companions. It then dawns upon him that the best way of escape from all these troublesome conditions would be to end one's own life, and thus commit suicide. He would then adopt some means or other and thus achieve his desired exit from the land of the living. Would this be a real escape?

Let us see whether the action has been correct. Is there no escape from the above confused state apart from suicide? It is accepted that only a spineless coward would attempt such a course of action. Such a person would be one bereft of any self confidence and character. A person whose mind has been shaped and influenced by Buddhism would never reach such a desperate mental state. Why does such a negative condition arise in the mind. It arises because of "avidya" or ignorance which prevents the correct understanding and realisation of things. The ignorance paves the way for greed and desire. Ignorance covers the truth. When greed impels desires that cannot be satisfied, the mind becomes agitated. The mind would get diffused like a heap of ash that had been disturbed by a stone thrown at it. When the mind is so diffused and disturbed, calm consideration and reflective thoughts become impossible. The disturbed mind seeks solace by arriving at wrong decisions. The mind seeks to achieve wrong objectives. In this agitation he seeks revenge if his thoughts and aims are thwarted. A great sense of jealousy spring up. Finally fear overtakes him. He would be so unsettled that he would not be able to stay quiet and composed in any one place. He would roam about in a confused state of mind. He would become agitated by constantly thinking about the loss that he had incurred. He would become isolated. Could such a mind be comforted by merely preaching the Dhamma to him. If he is lectured to and preached at, he would consider such, as his enemies. He would become angry and irritated at such people. What should then be attempted in such a situation. It has to be realised that this is a case of mental illness. It is a case of a person who gets ensnared in his own narrow world, and become sorely afflicted with his own tormenting thoughts. What must be attempted at first is to pacify the mind. This pacification cannot at this stage be done mentally because the patient is a mental patient. Therefore the pacification should be attempted through physical means. He should meet a physician and try and explain the conditions to him. If it is possible to have a deep sleep at this stage that would prevent the inflow of tormenting thoughts it would be very beneficial. What a doctor would do at this stage would be to prevent the inflow of tormenting thought processes even temporarily. The patient would be induced towards rest and sleep. Sedatives would be recommended. There would be various drugs and many tranquilisers would be administered that would naturally induce deep sleep. What the doctor has attempted here is the temporary stoppage of the inflow of disturbing thoughts. The tranquilisation of the mind that had been attempted through the administering of physical medicines and drugs, was attempted by the Buddha, through the power of the Dhamma and Meditation.

It was earlier explained that there are two sides or two components to everything existing in the world. The mind too has two sides or components that constantly interact on each other as it were. As much as there are disturbing and pain full concepts, there also are soothing and consoling concepts in the mind itself. When the tormenting thought processes are arrested the comforting and soothing thought process take predominance. It is at this stage that conditions would arise in order to avert the great calamity that would have occurred. This is the help that Buddhism affords at this point. It would be interesting to think of the Buddha's statement "Jata Sabbe Vinassanti"-"Everything that has arisen is destroyed". Also the fact "Sabbe Sankara Anicca" is significant "all component things break up". At this stage the contemplation or meditation on "Tri-Lakshna"-Anicca, Dukka and Anatta is very helpful. Before an explanation is given to the above meditation, it would be fruitful to consider the fact that with time, all things in the world change. Is there anything that remain without change in the world? Think of the vehicles, houses and property, the trees, the wealth of gems and gold, the sun and the moon, this great earth, all this will be destroyed at some time or other. By destruction is not meant the complete annihilation but a change from one state to another.

The mind too changes from moment to moment. So does the body. It too changes rapidly. There is the stage of coming into being, its existence and then the destruction, Everything is constantly be-coming and is constantly dying. What the "Tri Lakshana" Meditation illustrates, is that all component things break up. It is impermanent, it is unsatisfactory and it is ego-less. In that there is nothing that is unchanging and nothing not subject to change. This state has been explained in the previous articles and hence it would not be necessary to repeat the details again. But in brief it would mean that the so called body or "Kaya" is impermanent. Its condition is unsatisfactory. There is also no permanent self or soul that remain unchanged. The mind too has these three characteristics. Feeling is also the same. Consciousness too is characterised by the above three conditions. If as explained above every thing and every aspect of the world undergoes constant change, then how be it possible that only pain and anguish remain constant and without change. Why is it not possible, when any pain and anguish arise, to contemplate on the eternal fact that such pain and anguish is short lived and would pass away soon! Would that contemplation not give some relief to the tortured mind. If it be possible to wisely consider the fact that the anguish so arisen is of a temporary nature and would soon pass away that there would never arise situations where people would hastily rush to commit suicide and such rash actions. According to the fluctuations that occur in the mental states such feelings of joy or pain would soon pass away and be replaced by another. This is an almost universal truth.

There is a similar law in Economics which is termed as the law of availability. This law specifies that when something is consumed over and over again the desire to consume that thing diminishes with the regularity of usage. Let us take a very common example. A person with a packet of cigarettes has commenced to smoke. The pleasure he derives in smoking the first cigarette would be more than the pleasure he derives from the second. The satisfaction at the third would be even less. If he were to smoke continuously without a break he would reach a time when he has no desire for cigarettes at all. The condition of the mind is somewhat similar though working in the opposite direction. If a tormenting thought has entered the mind, and if it is not repeated and made to wind the mind over and over again, then with time that poignant feeling of pain would diminish. Then you have accustomed yourself to wisely bear the pain and thus relieve yourself of its poignancy, the mind automatically develops a sort of strength to withstand any assaults of pain and anguish. This state is similar to immunisation that is carried on in times of an epidemic. It is also wise to consider the fact whether an individual has the right to commit suicide when a great pain and anguish has assailed the mind.

Does the body belong to you. I have tried to explain in the earlier essays that according to Buddhism it has been proved that the body does not belong to an individual.

If the body is one's own it should obey and bestow to you only what is desired. There would then be no room for illness. There should only be happiness always. At whatever time it should not be terminated. All these examples point towards the universal fact that one has no right whatsoever to destroy a thing that does not belong to one. Such an action is against the law of the land as well. Let us also ponder on the fact whether unhappiness and suffering are ended by the act of suicide.

In the real sense suicide means the exchange for a set of disastrous painful circumstances, for another set of painful and disastrous circumstances, which are far more severe and ominous. Let us imagine the state of mind of a person attempting suicide. Is his mind full of monstrous or sublime considerations? Truly it would be in the opposite direction that the mind would work. The mind would be full of demeritorious thoughts of the lowest order. The thoughts would be as dark and tearful as the darkest pitch in a deep cavern. These dark thoughts would be full of anger, jealousy, envy, revenge and foul murder.

If the next birth of a person is conditioned by the thoughts uppermost at the dying moment, one could well imagine the state in which such a person would seek re-birth. This could be compared to a person who is in dire thirst would have drunk molten liquid to quench one's thirst. It could be compared to a person who is suffering from burns falling into a boiling cauldron of oil. When compared to that immense suffering and discomfiture on earth becomes very trifling. Such a person would naturally find existence in the four "apayas" or places of great discomfort which one termed as the four lower worlds. If according to Buddhism the mind is calmed and made still it would be possible to overcome any problem and confusion that may arise from time to time. Before taking any hasty and immensely foolish decision all were to calmly contemplate on the principles of Buddhism, it would be absolutely possible to escape from falling in to these states of distress. If you are able to make your mind a perfumed chamber where the Buddha constantly dwells, then it would be quite certain that you would remain steady and steadfast when faced with the various vicissitudes of life.

CHAPTER XVII

Those who weep and lament at death - are they the ones that do not die?

Why do people cry and lament on the demise of a close relative or dear friend? Is this action of lamentation correct. Is there any use in such lamentation. Today I would like to discuss this subject in some detail.

What is death. How does death occur. Let us look at this problem of death from the ordinary worldly angle as well as from a scientific view-point.

It is common knowledge that Buddhism is based on the principle of cause and effect. There is a plausible reason for every occurrence in the continuous reaction of cause and effect. The Buddha expounded the supreme truth that was manifest in the universe. He did not try to explain problems in the way he understood them. He explained in clear and precise terms the universal truth of cause and effect which directly affected all beings both human and divine. Before the concept of death is analysed it is interesting to see in a scientific way, the continuous reaction of forces that are always active in the universe.

The earth on which we live rotates at a speed of 1050 miles per hour. It is common knowledge that the earth revolves round the sun in 365 or 366 days. Further the earth along with all other bodies and constellations spin around the galaxy called the "Milky-Way".

In simple terms it spins like a whistle top on its own axis. While spinning it revolves around other objects as well. These two bodies further revolve around other bodies. The speed at which all these movements occur has been calculated. As said earlier the earth revolves round its axis at a speed of 1050 miles per hour. This would mean that during a short span of a second, it would have travelled at a speed of 1540 feet. So for the twinkling of an eye it would have travelled 1540 feet. If this can be seen by normal vision, that would be so stunning as to make a person faint off. Try and spin around at the speed of one foot per second and see the result. A person who has obtained mental poise through Bhavana and Meditation would be able to comprehend this concentric movement that is for ever present in the universe with a certain degree of clarity. It is this constant movement which is not discerned by normal vision, that prevents the true understanding of the universe as it really is. I would think that it is this constant movement which is the physical cause that acts as a thick mist that prevents the correct understanding of things as they really are. It is my conviction, that this continuous and incessant spin is also the scientific cause that makes human beings to be entangled in a net of delusion.

What is the other scientific result that is manifest by this continuous spin. It is the principle that at every moment everything in the universe changes by this movement. By change is meant the transformation of one state into another. There is a force that is generated by this continuous change. The force that is so generated by this regular spin is termed as gravitation or pulling towards each other. It is this gravitation that causes the spin, and further the spin causes gravitation. The cause becomes the result and the result becomes the cause.

Let us take a very simple example to illustrate this principle. Look at the electric fan that is in your home. If the blades are not cleaned, dust would collect on them. It is because of the revolving force that particles of dust are attracted towards it and settles on it.

In the final analysis the earth consists of dust, which has got together to form a mass. If the dust particles be broken up what would finally remain would be atoms which consist of electrons and protons. Finally it would be waves or ripples of force. These so called "waves" constantly vibrate. Then it would be seen that its the force of vibration that leads to the existence of matter. The vibration causes the formation of dust particles and in every particle of dust so collected the base remains as vibration. Things that are so collected, in the philosophical sense, have been termed as "Sankaras" or "formations" by the Buddha. When vibrational forces collate and form into a mass, the persistent and ever present condition is the state of vibration. This is a scientific truth.

What does this vibration result in? It results in the creation of a force. This force does not permit any mass or component thing to remain the same or stagnant for a long period of time. It is changed from one state to another state. In the real sense it then means that nothing is permanent. Therefore it is seen that there is nothing that can be termed as "Nitya" or unchanging. The Buddha realised the scientific truth that all component things do change and do not remain the same, 2500 years ago, through the Buddha's all seeing wisdom. After this short explanation of things let us look at the concept of Death and how it is related to all this.

A being from the time of his birth to the moment of death is invariably influenced and subjected to this process of change. Both the mind and body change according to this law. The mind which is intangible and not like the body which is tangible, is more susceptible and is influenced more by the universal spin that incessantly occur. The influence is more felt in the motives that arise in the consciousness or in the mind.

In the minutest division of consciousness, which is termed as "citta-kkhana" (consciousness-moment) is divided into sub divisions of the genetic (uppada) static (thiti) and dissolving (bhanga). Such was the Buddha's deep analysis of the mind. There is the continuous coming into existence and death-then death leading to existence again. Even if the world be destroyed at some time or other, the force that brings about change does not cease to exist. If by the exertion of some tremendous force, the sun, moon planets and other constellations collide with each other and is reduced to dust and ashes, yet the force of change or the continuous revolving and vibration force would not cease to be, Even if the physical world be destroyed yet in the dust that remains, there arises the condition of vibration. Due to this vibration, after the expiry of many million of years, the dust particles would gather together due this to vibration, and form a mass. This would be followed by other suns and other celestial bodies. This constant interplay of forces react on each other and this process goes on endlessly as it were.

In scientific terms it was Lavosior who discussed the principle enunciated as "matter cannot be created or destroyed". It is to explain this fact that it was said earlier that the force of vibration cannot be destroyed. This concept was further analysed by Albert Einstein (1879-1955) when in 1905 he explained that mass is equivalent to the force and vice versa. This established the universal fact that whatever force that is found in the world undergo changes but does not completely get destroyed. In earlier discussion I was able to explain this universal fact of change, as this salient fact had been completely comprehended by the Buddha and so well explained in the Dhamma. This universal law that subjects every component thing in the world to change and decay cannot ever be altered.

However developed and advanced scientific thought may be, yet it cannot go beyond this great universal law of change. Therefore it must be realised the fact of death can never be changed.

Let us examine how this universal law of change effect death. It had been explained earlier that mind changes rapidly with every conscious moment known as Citta-kkhana, such consciousness moments arise and then quickly pass away. They arise again only to perish. It has been said that every 17 consciousness moments the body condition arise and perish. They arise and pass away. In other words the body constantly changes. Even if one were to live for the maximum period of 120 years, yet during that period this process of change both of mind and body would have occurred many millions of times. We consider a person as dead, when the heat element and breath have left the mind and body. When it is said that they have left, it does not connote a complete destruction. One condition of life has been terminated in order to establish another condition of life. It is similar to the fact of vacating a house and going into occupation in another house. It would be possible for one to make this change of transition within any time from the time, that is at birth, or within any time of 100 or 120 years. The departure can occur at any point of time within this period. Sometimes this change occurs even while within the mothers womb. For others the change may occur at birth. To others the change may take place within a few days or months of birth. Or it may be within an year, two, three or ten or twenty or thirty or up to the maximum years aforesaid. The change indicates death. The death occurs according to the time limit that one one is entitled to or it may be caused by a vicious change in environmental considerations. That is quite a different matter about which we need not go into detail at the present moment. In this so called change of residence the responsibility should be borne by each person. When I mentioned various environmental changes, I was thinking of situations akin to earth quakes, conditions arising like the explosion of the atom bomb at Hisroshima and Nagasaki where many deaths occurred. These deaths cannot be considered as a direct result of karma, but have resulted through vicious environmental change. A being that is born to the world dies without even reaching a semblance of old age, as a result of the deeds done by him in his sansaric journey. This is because the individual had not collected the essential requirements that are required for a new existence. This matter had been discussed at length at a previous discussion. It means that he had failed to fill his travel-bag with what is most essential. What had been included are in-essential vipers. How many would have advised him then, as to what is essential and what is not. If he had listened to any religious teacher who would have given correct advice, he would not have been subjected to such a condition as caused by a shortened life. Whatever ill-deed had been performed, its results or vipaka will have to be borne some day. Let us consider for a few seconds the state of society at the present time. How much of advice is being offered constantly and continuously. Do not kill, do not sell intoxicating drugs. Do not partake of drugs and liquor. One may even stand on ones head and preach these things but to no avail. These misdeeds are performed not only by the so called uneducated class. This aspect is universal. One has got to reap what one has sown. Is it therefore correct to be perturbed when the results are manifest? Should they cry and lament on such occurrences? Lamentation should occur not at death but when one's child or relation is about to engage in some crime or other. It is at such a point, either by lamentation or any other form of action, that one should prevent the person from executing a dastard deed. By some means or other the sowing of seeds that would result in unhappiness and misery in the future, should be prevented at any cost. There are certain instances when even mothers or fathers encourage their off-spring to inflict wounds on others. How many instances are there, where parents enjoy the wealth brought in by their children, knowing very well that the wealth has been obtained by foul means, of robbing or even murder. If they really love their children would they act in such fashion. Such persons are really not parents but enemies.

When a person who has reached eighty or ninety years and then passes away, should that be an occasion for lamentation. With the approach of old age what is it that really happens. One's eyesight becomes weak. The limbs become unsteady. Hearing fails. It would not be even possible to attend to the normal daily ablutions. Apart from these one becomes affected with such diseases as high pressure. There would be diabetic conditions present. There would be arthritic conditions and stiffness of bones and joints. This entire body has now become decrepit. Of what use is existence now? In the Maha Parinibbna Sutta, the Buddha has described in detail the afflictions that he had to bear in old age. The description is heart-rending.

When this state is reached what is it that an ordinary human being should do. It would be best to cast aside the dilapidated form and go in search of a new life. The wise would make every effort to avoid the formation of life-form knowing very well the intense suffering endemic in such a state. Every effort should be made to eliminate the conditions that would lead for the renewol of another life-form. When an old dilapidated house is left behind and entry is made into a new residence, would that be an occasion for lamentation and grief, or would one rejoice at such a transformation?

It would be quite clear to an observer as to what attitude should be adopted at the demise of a virtuous person who had lived his life in a decent manner. Let us look at this situation from another angle. It had been explained earlier that the life-span on earth, when compared to the life spans in the celestial regions, would be so minute as to last only for a twinkling of an eye. The maximum life span on earth may be a hundred years or at the most one hundred and twenty years. When compared to the immense life span explained in cosmic concepts how infinitely small and minute would this maximum period of 120 years be?

In the ultimate sense when during a short life span, that had been such a succession of the conditions of genetic (Uppada), static (thiti) and dissolving (bhanga) taking place, then why is it that when finally the life-force leave the body, there is such lamentation and grief. The important thing to contemplate is this. The person who cries and laments on the death of a person today, may be dead tomorrow. Looking at such foolish people who cry and lament, it may be that such people would have come to the conclusion, that the dead person had been subjected to a condition that they would never experience. But it must be truly recognized, that as the small lump of clay that is always there at the top of a mushroom, the only inevitable thing for every-one, including those that lament and weep, is death at some time or other. In cosmic concepts of time when one passes away today or tomorrow or even in another 120 years, would not be of such significant difference. The fact is that death has occurred.

All these facts would invariably lead us to the conclusion that we have been caught up in a web of illusion or maya. Really we have been enmeshed in a wide tangle of such nets. If lamentation and grieving is considered correct then it would be best to grieve not at the demise of others but at one's own demise. What should be done wisely would be to contemplate on the words of the Buddha, and follow diligently the path that had been indicated by him.

"Appamado amatapadam - pamado maccuno padam

appamatta na miyanti ye pamatta yatta mata."

"Vigilence is an abode of eternal life, thoughtlessness is the abode of death. Those who are vigilant do not die.

The thoughtless are as if dead already"

It must be realised that the Buddha never lead people astray. Taking the fact into consideration every attempt should be made to lead a blameless life and thus pave the way for final emancipation. The Buddhas appear in the world because of their immense compassion for mankind, so that finally mankind could be saved from the immensely painfull sansaric existence.

CHAPTER XVIII

Illumination that dawns from understanding the concept of death

In my last article I tried to explain how futile and meaningless would be the action of a person who laments at the death of another, when that same condition of death, was his most certain inheritance. Would there be any use in lamenting and grieving at the demise of another person. Let us examine this question in some detail. Why do we so lament and cry. It is because of the mental agony. The sadness is caused by a feeling of pain and agony. Why does that pain and agony arise. It arises at the loss of an individual. This sorrowful condition arises of the feeling of a sense of loss to one-self. It becomes poignant as one has lost something that belongs to one-self.

What becomes most prominent in this instance is also the concept of self or ego. The concept of "I" and "Mine". There is no lamentation and grieving at the death of a person who is not known to each other. At the death of a foreigner, or of a non relative there is no lamentation.

The heat of the bon-fire is felt most when one is most close to the fire. The further one moves away the heat of the fire is felt less. In the same manner the poignancy of death is felt keenly if it had been a close relation who had passed away. If the deceased had been beneficial towards one and also in proportion to the age, the poignancy varies. If a person is caught directly in the fire the heat will be severe. In closest proximity the heat would be almost unbearable. Getting further away the heat would become less and less. If a youth has passed away the sadness would be acute. If a parent who had looked after the needs of a family had passed away, the poignancy of such departing would be intense. The death of a brother or sister would cause somewhat of a lesser pain of mind.

The poignancy felt at the passing away of aged parents would be certainly felt less than the passing away of a youth. It would thus be seen that where the relationship between the deceased and the living gets lengthened or when the benefits derived is lessened, then the sadness of parting gets proportionately diminished. This reveals one salient fact. At any demise the poignancy is relative to one salient fact. At any demise the poignancy is relative to the degree of attachment to self. In other words the sorrow is self-centered. It is sad to be separated from one's beloved kith and kin "Piyehi Vippayogo Dukkho" so said the Buddha.

Then there is no person called "I" or "mine". It would be futile to lament at the passing away of another person. This aspect had been explained in the previous lectures. When the news is heard of the demise of a very close relative the mind then would become agitated. This agitation arises mainly because of the sense of loss and desolation felt in the mind. One experiences a sense of loneliness, that compels feeling that one is lost in the world. If one were to closely pay attention to the type of wailing and lamentation that takes places in a funeral house it would become manifestly clear that the lamentation does not refer to the dead person but the lamentation refer to one-self. The purpose of such lamentation seems to me, with the object of obtaining some sympathy for oneself. The lamentations are mainly self-centered. This situation arises because of the great egoism that prevails.

On occasions like these, when death occurs, there appears an inner feeling and understanding that at any day in the future such a state would befall oneself. This feeling may not be a very prominent one on the surface, but underneath there seems to be such a lurking feeling. This underlying thought may cause a certain degree of fear. All these so called fears and ideas arise in the minds of un-initiated and ordinary human beings. One should not be blamed for harbouring such ideas. This is the normal human way of thinking.

This manner of thinking is due to the fact that human beings are enmeshed in a net of delusion, which clouds our existence. If the concept of death is properly understood, what happens at death, and how it is caused, then understanding would dawn that is the real sense death can be compared to a transference of residence, the movement from one house to another. I would like to pay a little attention as to how death is occassioned according to Buddhism.

On this matter there are two points of view among scholars. There is a point of view expressed that an individual at death, before he fixes upon the next rebirth stays or lives in an intermediate stage called the "Antara Bhava". The manner of leaving one state and establishing re-birth in another state, had been discussed in the earlier lectures and hence it would not be necessary to go into major details here. It has been explained how according to Kamma-vipaka, the arising of the patisandi-citta, then the Bhavanga Citta and the Cutti-Citta, determine the next existence. I too accept the view that determined by the result or vipaka of the good and evil actions performed, that consciousness that leaves the body at death find a suitable birth. Yet the question remains, whether this next existence is determined immediately the consciousness leaves the body at death or does the consciousness exist in an intermediary stage or Antara- Bhava, awaiting the correct moment to find suitable re-birth.

Those who accept the view point of the "Intermediate-stage" or "Antara-Bhava" maintain that consciousness remains in a temporary resting place for a few days or for a short period of time, until a suitable situation arises for re-birth. If this point of view is accepted let us examine how this situation becomes possible. If one were to find re-birth according to the manner of one's last dying thoughts, then certain factors should be satisfied for the fruition of such re-birth.

In the first instance then there should be a suitable background or environment made ready in the form of a place and a family that equates with the last thoughts of the Karmic vipaka. Then at that moment of passing away, a wife and husband of that particular suitable future family should have come together. Therefore that individual who would be re-born into that family, should have the background made ready to equate with his previous Karma that he had gathered. It is said that the Bodhi-Satva in his last birth which flowered into Buddha-hood, considered five salient points before conception in the human world. The suitability of the mother, the clan the area, the country and period of time were all taken into consideration so that the Buddha could flower in the correct and auspicious circumstances and absolutely suitable environment. However potent a seed may be, in order for it to grow and flower and bear fruit, the soil should be made suitable with sustenance of manure and water. This cannot be done hastily or in a haphazard manner, in a short period of time. If one were to think in the above manner, it would be quite logical to accept the theory of an "Antara-Bhava" or intermediate state of existence. It would be cogent to explain the concept of death as seen by a contemplative mind. How much this is in accordance with the Buddha's exposition, shall be discussed later.

What happens at death is the separation from the body of the thought process, that had been nourished by both meritorious and demeritorious Kamma. It can also be called the separation of the five-fold consciousness from the physical body.

To express in simple terms, meritorious and demeritorious Kamma can been explained as good and bad action. The deeds which are termed active and those that are negative. In whatever term this is explained, it expresses the two primary divisions that is manifest in the world. When a person engages in performing meritorious deeds, then the mind becomes sublimated and brightened. The opposite conditions are manifest with the performance of dark and negative deeds. Although in the true sense the mind cannot be really classified as the "bright side, and dark side", as the mind is intangible, yet these concepts are used in order to make the situation clear to the uninitiated person, so as to make comprehension easier. When engaged in good the mind gets illumined and becomes full of effulgence. The mind then acquires the positive characteristic of light. When dark deeds are performed the mind becomes clouded and musty. There is a concept of darkness, of heaviness. The mind looses its buoyancy. The mind then acquires the negative characteristics of darkness. Therefore the mind is constantly subjected to both these forces of good and bad. Each state becomes prominent in a greater degree or a lesser degree approximately to the frequency of the deed. This condition of the mind would remain as such, until an individual is able to reach the highest state of development at sainthood or Arahatship. This state would exist until the evil proclivities of mind, Loba, Dosa and Moha are completely eliminated from the mind. What happens at the moment of death is the separation of the mind or consciousness from the physical body. Consciousness or mind is termed as Nama, and the physical body is termed Rupa. The mind or consciousness has no physical characteristics and it is intangible. But the body is physical and tangible. The mind cannot be physically touched, but the body can be so touched. When it is said that the mind is separated from the body, it means that the body that had encaged the mind, has been released from the cage as it were. The mind or consciousness that has no physical characteristics, when once released from the body begins to act independently. It acts in the fashion of a bird that has been released. It would flap its wings and soar upwards to the sky. The released mind too behaves in a similar fashion.

The mind which had been subjected to myriads of changes (of Uppada-Tithi-banga) will find it impossible to exist without a physical form. When the life's breath has once left the body the mind or consciousness cannot remain in that body. The mind too must invariably leave the body. Our question would arise at this point. A person who has engaged himself in enjoying the fivefold sense pleasures in an indiscriminate fashion, with a great greed for wealth would find it difficult to depart leaving the body. How would it be possible to set aside easily all the wealth and possessions that had so painstakingly collected during his life time. He would therefore try to cling greedily to his wealth and children looking longingly at them. When the life-breath commences to leave the body, the mind would get attracted towards the wealth and the children and loved ones. Then there would be a contest as it were, the last breath trying to leave the body and mind longingly yearning for the worldly goods, that would be left behind.

It would be seen there would be a great struggle by the mind, that is bound by the desire for worldly goods, when the moment arise for the breath to leave the body. As the life-breath departs invariably this force will arise in the mind using much force, as the mind leaves the body. There would be a highly convulsive state. To a person who had been very closely attached to things worldly, this force would be felt as the crashing of thunder bolts. This is not a clash of thunder that can be heard by the physical ear, but is strictly a mental condition. To a person whose worldly desires have been lessened the impact of such a noise would be very little. According to the proportion of the kusal and akusal, good and bad deeds performed, this explosive feeling would be less or more. The mind will experience such a state because of the fact that during one's span of life on earth all impressions and feelings have been experienced by the mind.

When the mind or consciousness has left the physical body the great confusion that arise in the mind is because the mind becomes unable to control the various feelings that arise. When the individual was alive, the various feelings and emotions that arose were controlled by the mental factor. By "mental factor" is meant the functioning of the brain. This brain functioning made the individual to think and come to conclusions. What happens on the death of an individual, is that function which was performed by two agencies, is left now at death to be performed by one agency. That one agency is the mind or consciousness. Hence the power of selection and discrimination disappear. The mind accepts any impression that comes to it in the way it has arisen, without discrimination or selection. In this instance the mind becomes enfeebled. It accepts everything that comes into its preview as would be like a little child in all its innocence. At the time consciousness leaves the body, if there be a suitable environment made ready, the consciousness would take root in that environment in the manner of an embryo.

When there is no such suitable environment ready, in order for the consciousness to exist, it is essential to have a physical body. Has the consciousness or mind the necessary ability to create such another physical body the moment it leaves the previous existence? It is at this moment another set of forces come into operation, almost instantly. The mind that has left the physical body immediately take the characteristics of its original state. Here the mind has meritorious, de-meritorious and transcendental qualities inherent in it. The meritorious is the effulgent side. De-meritorious is the dark side. Transcendental side abounds in purity and light. These conditions of the mind change at immense speed from "uppada" to "tithi" and then to "banga". This ever-changing consciousness needs a body to continue its existence. The mind selects the form of the body that it has used during the lifetime. As this form of the body has been improved in the consciousness then a mind-created form comes into existence,. In order for the continued existence of this "mind formed" body certain physical conditions are necessary. This necessity is fulfilled by the finest and almost imperceptible physical attribute that is ever found. This is none other than the vibrational waves that are manifest in the entire universal space.

The mentally created form, consists of these very fine vibrational waves. From where did these vibrational waves come from? It had been explained earlier that the minutest speck of dust when finally analysed consists of waves of energy. It is these "waves" that contribute towards the formation of the mind created form. This condition would be somewhat similar to the appearance of pictures on the television screen, which originally had been transmitted to the centre through television waves. In this instance there is no tangible form that can be touched. The mind-form that comes into being in the "intermediatory" or "Antara-bhava" is also similar in character.

Here the mind is constantly influenced in a competitive manner by the good and bad done in previous lives in the manner of lightning. These conditions become manifest because the mind has left the physical body, and the physical body has no influence on the mind. To a person whose defilements have not been completely eliminated, the path to Nibbana is obstructed and the effects of good and bad Kamma begin to manifest. Greed and attraction pave the way for the arising of a new state of existence. There is a sense of attachment and clinging. As the original unblemished state of mind too comes forward to a certain degree, there is a wonderful mind force that is collected. What makes full use of this force is the condition called "Uppada" or the concept of clinging fast. What happens here the attraction of the mind, to the core force of the atom and making use of that vibrational force for the formation of the "Mind-form". What could have happened in this instance is the making use of a physical force that is manifest in the entire universe though that physical force be so fine as to be even invisible, being used in a temporary fashion for the formation of a body. Such a temporary formation is made necessary because for the formation of a fully physically constituted body a period of time is essential. What has happened here is the fact that the time, factor is insufficient for a normal conception to take place and for the formation of a truly physically constituted body. The mind has absorbed the finest matter available in the universe and thus formed a so called temporary or "intermediate body," or an Antara-Bhava.

CHAPTER XIX

Dying unconscious and arising of the last thought process

What was attempted in the last article was to explain the condition that would arise, if no immediate conception took place and the experience that CONSCIOUSNESS would undergo at a so called temporary halting place. In other words what was attempted was to explain the workings of the mind in such an interim state prior to a fixed re-birth in Sansara. What would be the experiences felt by the mind in such a state. What would be its scientific basis. Some scholars would explain the aforementioned state as the "Antara-Bhava" or interim or temporary existence. This condition which is entirely "mind-made" was termed as "Atman" or "Soul" by the Hindus, who did not really appreciate this mind made condition. What the Hindus called "atman" was the essence that left the body along with the last "life-breath". Therefore they described this state thus:- "It cannot be divided. It cannot be burnt. It cannot be made wet. It cannot be dried up. It is permanent. It spreads everywhere. It is unchanging it is firm. It is ancient." All these descriptions were proffered after perceiving this mind made body. They explained its condition in the above fashion as they were unable to appreciate and comprehend the real structure and condition. As they did not possess supreme knowledge they were led astray regarding, the true understanding of this "mind made existence". They mistakenly asserted that this condition had an essence. They mistakenly asserted that this condition had a permanent soul. It was the Buddha who with his transcendental

149

wisdom saw the true condition as to what really happened when consciousness, along with the life breath left the body at death. The Buddha very explicitly stated that at death a person does not take away anything at all, except the results of the positive and negative Karma, that had been performed during the life time by the individual concerned. The Buddha saw this condition through his para-normal wisdom and expressed this supreme truth in clear terms. What was carried on from existence to existence was not a physical essence, but a continuous thought process which had been termed as a "Santati" in Buddhism.

There is a western film called "ghost" that is being shown here presently. This film is based on the concept of a transmigrating soul or entity. I think this has taken as its base the Hindu concept of rebirth. The film stresses on the emergence of a soul from the dying physical body.

At death, when a mental image is formed to which the cosmic vibrations gets attracted to, could this phenomena be termed as a soul? Could an illusionary form, composed of vibrations be divided into sections? Could it be burned.? Could it be moistered? Could it be dried up? Could it be touched? Could it be so diffused at every place? Is it something permanent? Does it never change? Although the Buddha was able to completely dispel this false concept of things, yet the Brahamin establishment did not agree to give up this false idea they had cherished for thousands of years, as it would completely destroy the basis from which they derived very existence and other privileges. The Brahamin class therefore preserved this soul concept with diligence, as it was so conducive for their uninterrupted existence.

If the mind created body that is composed of waves of virbration, on the demise of an individual, could be considered as something permanent and unchanging, then it would be correct to consider forms that appear on Television also as permanent and unchanging. It would be correct to state that Arhants and those who have reached transcendental heights in mind development and those beings with three noble root conditions (Tihetuka patisandhi) at the break up of the body and at death, would not find it necessary to spend an interim period in an intermediate state or :"Antra-Bhava". The Arhants at death immediately attain supreme Bliss or Nibbana. Those who have attained great transcendental heights of meditation, would at death be immediately be re-born, in the Rupa or Arupa worlds. Those who die with the three noble root conditions, would be re-born in Deva worlds. The intermediate state or "Antara-Bhava" would only be necessary for those whose merits have proved to be insufficient. Who are these individuals who are termed or classified as "Tri hetuka". This category of individuals have to a very great extent diminished the evil proclivities of the mind. It is those whose mental condition of Greed, Anger and Ignorance have been reduced to a very great degree. To express this fact in another way would be to say that those individuals with great merit who have cultivated the concepts of selflessness and liberality, compassion and wisdom. It is those whose positive characteristics have been greatly increased and the negative side has been diminished. It is those whose mental attitudes have developed effulgence and whose dark concepts have almost completely diminished.

Let us now consider what happens at the moment of death. When death approaches the consciousness and life breath prepare to leave the physical body. It has been established that even for a person who had remained unconscious at this moment there arises an element of consciousness.

There is a reason for the arising of such a mental condition. How do we gauge that a person is quite conscious. It is through the operation of the sub-conscious state. I think this statement needs a further clarification. It would be easier to understand this condition if we were to consider how when living a person would have shaped his thoughts from topic to topic. It had been explained earlier that there are so called six doors through which impressions are taken in. It is through the eye, the ear, the nose, the tongue, the body and consciousness that impressions enter the body. If one were to consider the workings of each of these so called "doors", it would be easier to understand the thought process of a dying individual. There is an inherent force that is incorporated in to each of these doors, that make it possible for each door to recognize each thought process that enter through such doors. In the classical Buddhistic explanation each such force is explained as "Chakku-Vinnana" or eye visaul) consciousness, pertaining to the "eye-door" "sota vinnana" or ear consciousness for the "ear-door" and so forth for the remaining entrances or doors. Therefore thoughts and impressions that enter through each door or entrance has been given the particular name through which these impressions enter. Therefore it will be seen that consciousness is part of the mind process and this force arises dependent upon the entrance or door through which it has entered. When such an impression enters from whatever be the entrance, and when such an impression transforms into a thought process, many changes occur in an extremely rapid fashion.

When this process is understood in respect of the eye, impressions strike on it and eye consciousness arises. Then there arises a process of recognition. After this there arises a so called thought process which culminates into a "thought-action" process which can be termed as "Cetana" or Karma-formation. In simple terms it means that the tongue recognises taste, the nose recognises smell, the ear recognises sound and finally the mind recognises a thought process. In this instance although the mind too take on impressions, yet it does not react in the same manner as the other "doors" by coming in direct contact with an object. I tried to explain this process in somewhat detailed manner, in order to emphasise that when a person is alive, a thought process does not arise in the mind directly, but only through the impressions that find entrance through the other five "doors" or entrances mentioned earlier. An impression first strikes at the relevant entrance, and then a thought process occurs. It is also important to realise that when an impression enters through the relevant door, and consequently a resulting thought process occurs, its potency is somewhat reduced. When such a thought process enters the mind of a living individual, there is a process of analysis and discrimination that occurs. This analysing process leads to certain decisions that are arrived at by the mind. Say for example if a deep concept of sorrow has entered the mind through a relevant entrance at that moment a living individual is able to consider that deep sorrow with a degree or equanimity and thus in a way to reduce the impact of such deep sorrow. It is necessary to stress the fact that this process of equanimity could only be possible to a person when he is alive. There is no such discernment of equanimity by a person who is about to die. What then happens to this force that was associated with the five senses. Do they completely disappear? There is a physical law of nature that states that a force or mass, cannot be created or destroyed. It is interesting to ponder upon this scientific axiom. If such a force does not die off completely what then happens to it? It is correct to infer that such a force would get "attracted" to that along which it always existed and by which it had earlier depended on and come into existence. Then it becomes quite apparent that the force would attach itself to the mind of the dying individual at the moment of death when the mind separates itself from the physical body, with which it had been continuously associated with the above mentioned force gets linked up with the mind and gets absorbed into the mind as it were. It is this force which is associated with the mind that leaves the body at death which is termed "Pancha-Upadana Skanda" which can strictly be expressed as the five fold groups of existence which form the objects of clinging. This force cannot get eliminated or migrate to another place. If this force were to get eliminated or disappear for ever, then when another being takes conception, there would not be an opportunity for mental impressions to manifest and take root. It will thus be seen that when a new individual comes into being, this force that had been earlier associated with the mind, gets once again attracted towards the stream of consciousness or "Vinnana".

What had been attempted above was to explain in somewhat detailed manner, that at death, that the activities that had been previously performed by the five sense organs have been taken over by the mind. In other words the force that had been associated with the five senses have now been absorbed by the mind. Therefore it would now become clear that immediately after death, when a mind-formed intermediate state comes into existence, that mind-formed intermediate state has the power to take in impressions. When a seemingly unconscious person passes away, and the five sense doors do not function, yet that function of taking on impressions can be performed by the mind. This can be compared to a dream state. In such a-dream state the sense-doors do not function. Yet the mind performs the task of the sense doors and hence the vivid impressions visualised in the dream. It could be stated that in a dream-state the sub-consciousness is awake, and active. It is because of this state that a dream can be remembered later. Even if the sub-conscious state is awake or not, yet the normal mind is always active when the sub-conscious state becomes less active, the process by which the mind functions is forgotten. Therefore even in a so-called unconscious state the innermost undercurrent forming the condition of a "being" the "Bhavanga-Citta" can manifest itself as a "Chuti-citta" death consciousness or a "Patisandi-citta" rebirth consciousness, as the occasion demands.

Let us pause for a moment here and turn briefly to a subject about which a detailed explanation would occur in the following chapters. If according to the teaching of the Buddha, the last thoughts of a dying person condition his next existence or re-birth, how does an "individual" who would have been in an intermediate state or "Antara-Bhava" determine its re-birth? It had been stated earlier that at the moment of death, a great effort or force is necessary to separate the mind from the physical body. The last thought process is always accompanied by an intense force. A question may be posed here as to what thought process would have a resultant effect, the one accompanied by a force, or one bereft of such a force. The dying flame of a lamp flickers with an intensity, that burns itself out completely. The dying force draws all its energies out and burns brilliantly. Even at death such a situation becomes evident.

An "Antara-bhavika" who has created a mind-made body and had existed for a whatever period of time when a real re-birth takes place, it becomes absolutely certain that it is always the force that accompany the last thought that would really condition the next existence.

The consciousness or mind of an "Antara-Bhavika" function in a very simple and tender manner, somewhat according to the working of the mind of a child. This is due to the fact that when living, the mind is controlled by the brain as well as by the five senses. Such restraint and control are absent in the above state. It is quite evident that a force that strikes direct is felt more effectively than a force that strikes after deflection. In such an intermediate stage as the feeling and impressions strike directly without any deflection, the force is felt more keenly and fiercely.

CHAPTER XX

Getting caught in enemy traps and drinking molten - lava

Explanation as to how a person at death would be re-born in an intermediate stage or "antara-bhava" was amplified in earlier chapters. In this chapter it would be attempted to explain the suffering that would have to be endured in such a state.

It was noted that at death, consciousness would depart from the physical body. What would accompany the mind or conscious at such a moment? It would be correct to state that the mind would take away with it all things that are connected with the mind. It was also explained earlier that the mind along with the power or ability to take in impressions is also associated with the mind at the moment of death. What else does the mind gather to itself at the moment of departure. The evil roots of greed, anger and delusion are also associated with it. Then there are the positive characteristics of liberality, compassion and wisdom too. All the tendencies and characteristics that have accrued in to the consciousness accompany the mind. It is interesting to note that these tendencies both positive and negative that have been adhering to it throughout the perpetual wandering or round of rebirth (Sansara) accompany the mind at such a stage of departure. If the aforementioned tendencies had been obliterated would it be possible to discover the conditions for another existence or re-birth. It is this long accrued tendencies that provide the fuel for the further travel in sansara. During the immensely long journey much of the fuel may have been exhausted, and much fuel may have been added. It is this force that propel the individual in the long sansaric journey, experiencing much unhappiness and suffering,. These tendencies can also be termed as kusal or akusal kamma or meritorious or demeriorious kamma. Each individual would at some time or other arrive at the time when the result of such action has to be experienced. It is necessary to prepare for such an occasion. It is necessary to recall the fact that positive or meritorious kamma, had been earlier explained as shining non-heavy, with great lustre but yet it is impermanent and changing. Demeritorious kamma can be characterised as heavy, dark, non-lustrous are also impermanent and changing. It is only Nirvana that is absolutely shining full of lustre and non-changing.

The five fold hindrances or obstacles, that cross the mind, that blind the mental vision and the various meritorious and demeritorious kamma act as stumbling blocks to one on the path to Nirvana. These cover the path to progress and the path becomes difficult. This can be compared to a set of giants who have covered a very precious object, there by preventing its possession by any other aspiring person. The mind that leaves the body is accompanied by all these above mentioned tendencies. To explain this idea further such a mind would compose of meritorious and demeritorious tendencies, good and bad kamma, and even of powerful tendencies that lead to the realisation of Nirvana. The mind or consciousness that leaves the body at death, spin with great speed, and for its stability create a very temporary mind created "body". At such a stage what is significant is this. The mind which at every moment change at tremendous speed (uppada-titi-banga) tend to act as if without any control. Whatsoever terndencies both good and bad, positive and negative tendencies that have been collected through an immensely long period of time, become activated continually and move at an immense speed. To an individual who has amassed demeritorious kamma, what arise is an abyss of darkness consisting of pain, suffering and fear. There arise uncertainty, disgust and burning

To a person who has accrued much merit, the situation that presents itself is quite the contrary. As a gentle and perfumed breeze that comes towards him, there float towards him a great effulgence, a halo of light. There is a feeling of comfort and happiness. There is peace, contentment and light.

It is important to realise that an individual when alive performs both meritorious and demeritorious deeds. It is a mixture of both varieties of deeds. An individual may have performed very meritorious deeds at some time in Sansara, and the resultant good may appear foremost, temporarily subduing the bad kamma that has so far accrued. As such at death such an individual sees an effulgence. He tries to go towards that light and follow it earnestly, but finds that he has not sufficient force or energy to proceed towards the light that he has perceived. The reason for such a situation is that the good results of kamma cannot overcome the predominantly strong evil effects that had gathered much force in time. The evil last thought has been a very strong influence that had penetrated and percolated deeply into the consciousness. To a person who had accrued much merit, even if there be traces of darkness that appear as a result of the previous bad kamma performed yet the good kamma is so strong as to push back the evil effects and not allow such evil proclivities to take even temporary predominance. The mind that has now left the body with a certain amount of ease, moves freely without much obstruction. It is even possible for such a mind to even temporarily conceive Nirvanic Bliss. The bliss and effulgence that is experienced in such a state is so supreme, that it is not possible to explain it in ordinary words. This blissful condition is also constantly subjected to a continous state of "Uppada, Thiti and Banga".

The mind in such a state had become free of sense impressions and control from physical defects. Hence the mind often and on revert to its original resplendent state. Mind's original characteristic is Bliss. This Bliss is characteristic of the Nirvanic mind. Although this is the pure original unblemished state of the mind, the ordinary individual is unable to reach this state or realise its beauty, as the mind is constantly covered by evil proclivities and the five-fold obstacles (Nivarana) delusion, greed and such other impure things or dhammas.

The mind in such a situation as it is free from the troubles of physical bondage, and not subjected to such control, often and on is able to get a glimpse of nirvanic brilliance. But it fails to pursue the path towards that brilliance, due to the persistent desire for existence and to the stubborn desire for physical pleasure. The mind that had been accustomed to the enjoyment of such pleasures, always seem to be drawn towards them, due to the continuous mixture of good and bad deeds that had been performed. The mind is continuously drawn towards celestial pleasures as well as worldly comfort and happiness. As was said earlier, although traces towards Nirvanic bliss arise, yet it remains rather weak and not persistent enough to break away from stronger forces that result from meritorious and demeritorious deeds. The force from such deeds exert a stronger pull or attraction.

It is interesting to ponder on what the so called being in the intermediate state or "Antara-Bhava" experiences. What do those experiences signify. The experience of darkness is symbolic of the lower states of suffering, states where beings experience unsatisfied desires, that state of Asuras or Titians, who are always enveloped in anger and the animal states. The bright diffused light indicated earlier represent the heavenly realms, the human states. The unimaginable non-expressible beauteous lustre would indicate the concept of Nirvana.

Let us now turn towards the feelings that are experienced by those in the aforesaid intermediate state of existence. When the mind had left the physical body, it feels as it had been released from bondage, as freed from a cage. It becomes then freed from the physical bondage that it had been subjected to for such a long period of time. The opportunity now arises for the mind to act freely and without restraint. This situation arises as there is no agent to control the mind. The mind gets freed and clear of the discerning and discriminating concepts. When alive the mind was subjected to the discerning functions of the brain of separating good from the bad there was the power of discernment. The mind was further controlled and influenced by the impressions that came in through the five-fold sense organs. Earlier when the tongue experienced a taste, it could decide, as to its bitterness, sourness, sweetness and also the power to discern as to its poisonous nature or as to its beneficial nature. There was this manifold ability for the mind to gauge to measure or to discern. Does the mind in the above state also have such power of choosing and separation? If the mind still had the power of discerment it is due to the fact that the instruments that were responsible for such discernment still would have some influence. It is therefore important to realise the fact that although the organs of impression formation are non-existent in the present state, yet their former influence is still being borne at sub-conscious level. To express it more precisely the intermediate being would take in all impressions directly and without any attempt at selecting, choosing or rejection. This state would be comparable to the mind of a child who normally would have no power of discernment or discrimination. As such a feeling of happiness or sorrow would have a direct impact, and hence its force would be stronger than usual.

Why is it that on the demise of a person, meritorious deeds are performed and alms are offered consisting of such foods as were liked by that particular individual when alive? It is felt that the "Intermediate being " or "Antara-bhavika" on the sight of such food partakes of it, not in the physical sense of taking the food into his hands as such. The sight of food that it relished brings about a mind made element of satisfaction. This attitude of mental satisfaction is possible as the subconscious state (Vinnana) has planted itself deep in the recess of the mind.

It is interesting to note that in most village homes, "Vessantara Jataka" is recited continually for seven days after demise of a person. This custom is practiced as there is a belief that the departed person would be there in an "Intermediate state" and would take in the recital in a direct and forceful manner. Then a meritorious thought process would be generated. The mind would be satisfied and happy. It is in this fashion that the "Antara-Bhavika" takes in all impressions and feelings, both of happiness and pain.

What is the condition of an individual who has passed away after committing a heinous deed. Let us for a moment consider the case of a suicide bomber who has destroyed many lives and in the process eliminated his own life as well. There is also the case of criminals who after the elimination of many other lives take a capsule of cyanide to avoid being taken in by the law officers. would he thus escape from the trammels of law? But could such an individual escape from the inexorable laws of karma? Such a person would be experiencing a great hatred before the perpetration of the dastard deed. His last moments would be overflowing with hatred. Thoughts of revenge and hatred would be uppermost in his last thought process. He would become enveloped in a film of darkness and misery, flames of hatred as would arise from a great conflagration would surround him, and explosions of dreadful and fearful sounds would envelop him. The petrol of hate, revenge and anger, would ignite with a tremendous force.

Let us now turn to something quite practical. Imagine a moment when fear and thought of imminent death would assail you or think of a situation when an almost unbearable pain would strike you in some vital part of the body. Let us think of even a worse situation when a dreaded fire has encompassed your entire body. Such situation would be most fearful, would be most dreaded. In such a situation, the brain would re-act quickly and try to adopt some form of action to minimise the awful situation and bring it under control. Imagine a situation where such control would be quite impossible. Such a situation could not be expressed in words. Such torment does not end. Such torture is continuous. It arises, it ceases, but again to arise with greater intensity. It is a dreaded continuous process.

To end this pain there is no short cut method of the cycnide capsule. If such a person who had perpetrated such a crime and subsequently endure unending torture of mind were to return to earth, would he spare that individual at whose instance and inducement the crime had been perpetrated? This great torture would it end in a day or two? Or would it end in a hundred years, or two hundred, or even a thousand years? Who can gauge the length of such immense travelling in Sansara.

Buddhist literature has pointed reference to places of great suffering termed as hells. Is not such suffering akin to the gulping of Moltan lava. If one were to contemplate for a moment this immense degree of suffering, when one is alive, one would never be inclined towards the perpetration of evil or the performance of dastard crimes.

CHAPTER XXI

At the moment of death, is it light or darkness that is experienced ?

You would now fully realize the fact that the re-becoming or re-birth of an individual in the next existence is due to or more correctly conditioned by results of his actions in the previous births. But this fact shall not make us come to the conclusion that there is permanent soul or being that transmigrate from one birth to the next. This re-becoming is strictly caused and influenced by the results of the good and bad Karma performed in the course of Sansara or round of births characterised by perpetual wandering. As the actions performed by an individual in the present existence has a direct influence on the condition of life in the next birth, he has to bear direct responsibility for such actions either good or bad. Let us now delve a little into the conditions that prevail and would have to be faced by an individual at the moment of death.

A person may breath his last very quickly, almost with a passing of a second as it were. Another, would struggle hard at breath and the final end would come after the lapse of a considerable length of time. Another person would be on the verge of death, between two worlds as it were for a number of days and then recover a little, only to pass away again in a few days. There would be the case of another who would be struggling for breath for a number of days, struggling to die as it were, causing great distress not only to himself but even to others who are his near relatives.

Why do such different conditions manifest? It would be quite correct to assume that the above conditions are relative to the results of the actions performed during the particular life time.

This condition is also relative to the manner that the mind had been fashioned during the life time. A person whose mind has been well ordered, whose words, thoughts and deeds have been made very positive and thus have developed a sense of lightness of mind, at moment of death, has naturally been prepared for such an inevitable situation. The mental pictures that appear to him at the moment of death are all pleasant characterised by light and effulgence. The place of next birth is indicated and he begins to realise that his re-birth would take place in a state which is more satisfactory than the state which he is about to depart. The attractions that had drawn him to this world now become less rigid. It is true to say that it is somewhat difficult to break away from the bonds that have been cultivated for a long time towards one's wife and children members of the family like brothers and sisters, towards wealth and property. It is equally difficult to lay aside the concepts of 'I and mine' that had grown because of ignorance and the persistent film of darkness that covers the ultimate true condition of things. How could it be possible to leave behind all these considerations and depart alone.

To an individual who has performed continuous meritorious deeds in his life-time and to those who have cultivated their minds through meditational exercises, the effulgence or light that he perceives at the moment of death, makes it possible for him to forget all the aforesaid attractions. The light and effulgence so attracts his mind that all other considerations become of no importance or significance. There is a growing desire towards the new state that is being indicated by that great light. His mind draws towards that and he feels that the new state is far more satisfactory than the state which he is now departing. Therefore the mind earnestly tries to follow the path indicated by light. As the last breath leaves the physical body the conciousness too leaves the body and finds a new existence. At this stage according to the last impulsive thought process (Javana Citta) re-birth conciousness arise. The individual who had consistently performed meritorious deeds in proportion to the strength of such actions, finds re-birth in the Deva Worlds or in human existence, or any such fortunate state. There is a persistent belief that if a suitable state of re-birth is not quite available the departing being spends a short period of time in an intermediate state or 'antara-bhava'. When conditions become ripe for such a state of re-birth, the intermediate stage is quickly given up and re-birth takes occurance.

Let us for a moment consider the situation that would have to be confronted by an individual at the the moment of death, whose prior life had been full of misdeeds and who had engaged himself in the grossest forms of physical pleasures paying emphasis to his views that there is no after life, and there is nothing to be worried about after death. While living such a person had paid attention to only the negative side of things, to actions that could be classified as de-meritorious. His mind or consciousness had been heavily weighted by darkness heaviness and all such negative characteristics. Could it ever be imagined that at the moment of death such a being would move towards light and brightness. Brightness and darkness is not a condition that is manifest from outside. Such conditions arise from the mind itself according to the traits so cultivated while living. When greed and avarice have been predominent characters such conditions come to the fore-front. Then there is an element of clinging. Clinging for what? A strong persistent clinging becomes manifest for all that had been so stingyly collected and hoarded. A clinging towards the concept of 'I and mine' comes very prominently to the forefront.

An object that had been attracted towards a magnet can be separated only by using a certain amount of physical force. What are these conditions that are considered to be 'I and mine'. These denote none other than the wealth that had been greedily accrued during a long period of time. Perhaps it may be that this so called wealth had been collected after giving much un-happiness to others. This wealth may have been collected during one's lifetime by the sale of drugs and narcotics. It may also be that the wealth had been collected by a well organized ring or cartels. It may also be the wealth collected by the illicit cutting down of valuable trees which in the long run bring about disaster to natural environmental conditions. All the aforesaid wealth had been collected by various illegal means. When the final moments arrive for departure, longing thoughts linger on bringing to memory the past life that is quickly fading. There is an urgent longing for the wealth that is being left behind and a bitter remorse would arise in the mind when it is seen that it would be the others and not the collector of the wealth who would really enjoy such wealth. There would be tremendous remorse When such a person realizes that because of the enormity of crimes committed there would be no more peace or a period of enjoyment and satisfaction. The above would be the type of thoughts that would fleetingly pass through the mind of a person who has committed such ill deeds in this life. Altogether there will be a tremendous effect for the last breadth to leave the body, yet the mind finds itself attracted and longs greatly to the wealth that had been notoriously collected. There is no other world to him other than the wealth and desire for it. Although there is a great effort for the breath to leave the body, yet the mind or consciousness like an animal that is taken to slaughter, always draws back and thus gets fixed and attracted towards the wealth and children that inevitably would have to be left behind. To a person who had led a virtuous life whose wealth has been gathered in very righteous manner, such a dire and desperate situation would not arise at death.

The non-virtuous person at such a moment gets entangled as it were on two sides. On one side his desires attract him towards life. On the other side a strenuous effort is being made for the last breath to leave the physical body. The death drawl goes on for days for those individuals who have been greedily attracted towards the world with sensual desires. Such a condition may even be the lot for virtuous people, who have been greatly attached towards children and family. It can also be due to function of bad evil Karma of the past. It can safely be assumed that a great delay is experienced by those who are closely attracted to worldly conditions, when the time arrives for the mind to leave the physical body. What are the final visions that appear at such a moment to one who had constantly practised evil deeds. If for whatever reason a remembrance of a good deed done in this life or in any past existences, does not come to the mind's attention, then what would really come forward would be the thought of all the evil deeds performed and the signals that would appear would be of a disastrous and hedious nature. This would be similar to great darkness. A fearful chasm would appear before the mind's eye. Awful and fearful scenes would present themselves before the minds' eye. He would thus get a glimpse and become aware of the disaster that awaits him.

Such an individual would be quite reluctant to proceed on this destined journey. The reluctance is due to the fact that he has an instinct of the disaster that awaits him in the future life. To some due to a confusion of thoughts the inauspicious future is seen as somewhat auspicious and wholesome. To him the disaster is reckoned as something worthwhile and welcome. As such in his confused state he gets attracted to such a state. To some who get a momentary glimpse of the future awe-ful state the present state which he lived and is about to depart would seem as a very heavenly abode. It is these individuals that linger long drawing their last breath as it were for days on end.

Is it correct for those who witness these last stages to weep and lament aloud at the iminent departure of their loved ones. This is an important matter that should be discussed. If those around the death-bed wail and cry aloud in anguish, in my opinion it would cause greater difficulties for the one who is struggling to depart. When the departing person hears this loud wailing, it would invariably disturb his state of mind and further confuse him. Even if an attempt had been made by him to attain some serenity as the breath is leaving, such loud crying would certainly disturb his aforesaid serenity and confuse him at this very vital moment. Generally wailing and weeping is manifest when disaster strikes. The departing individual would also come to the conclusion that the wailing he hears is due to some great disaster that is about to occur. When such a thought process arise invariably the mind or consciousness would be subjected to much disturbance. There would be fear and consternation. The loud wailing would ultimately result in the departing individual turning away from the light that he had tried to go after with difficulty, and looking back at this great disturbance caused by wailing relations. He would definitely feel that departing is not a good thing. He would get attracted to his former life conditions. At such a moment the clear vision would be obstructed by a dark cloud that would pass across his mind. In such a condition, when the last thoughts arrive they necessarily would be characterised by a negative nature. It would thus be almost impossible for him to establish a fortunate re-birth. It would be inevitable disaster. It would be then realised that relatives that weep and wail at the bed-side of a departing individual will cause immense harm and dis-service. There is no doubt about this.

If there be wailing and lamentation at the demise of a person whose whole life had been characterised by both evil thoughts and dastard actions, the situation described earlier would be very much worsened. He who had been destined to be re-born in a place of somewhat minor distress, would be directed to a state of complete misery and absolute suffering this individual who had been assailed by tormenting and fearful visions, when the wailing is heard, the fearful and frightening visions would be experienced with greater intensity. The mind would be enormously perturbed, He would associate the awful wailings as part and parcel of the tormenting visions that had been experienced. He would then begin to realise that he would be falling inevitably into a great pit of darkness and misery, from which it would be almost impossible for him to extricate himself.

At such a critical occasion what is it that should be done apart from wailing and lamentation. As explained earlier there is in the world always conditions of good and bad, of merit and demerit. Even a person who had habitually been addicted to unskillful and de-meritorious acts, would have, however rarely it may be, performed some good. Therefore at the moment of passing away, what the relations or friends should do, would be to recall to his mind and bring back remembrance of the good action that had been performed. Such discussion should be repeated aloud and clearly. In the alternative it would be very beneficial if some religious text is read aloud. A Bhikku or Priest could be summoned for the performance of some religious rite or other that would influence the mind of the departing person.

The dying individual could thus be induced to follow the path of light and avoid the road that leads to darkness. If continually this exercise is performed till the final life breath leaves the body, it would be quite possible for the individual's last thoughts to be so influenced, that his re-birth conciousness would find establishment in a place of happiness and bliss. It is interesting to note that our elders had completely understood the significance of such acts and had very scrupulously adhered to such performances.

It had been the treasured custom of our elders to very carefully maintain a book which had a record of all the good deeds performed by them in their lifetime. I have seen with my own eyes how they would often and on read such accounts of their meritorious deed and derive much mental satisfaction. It was an established custom in the village that when the moment of passing away arose they would very clearly and loudly read the accounts that had been so written so that the dying individual's thoughts would be directed to such recitation. Although at that time long ago, I did not fully realise the value and significance of such action, now in the present time, I could fully appreciate and understand the intrinsic value of such a noble action. To a person who is familiar with the

Dhamma and had constantly practiced meditational exercises and thus cultivated the positive characteristics, there would never be any cause to fear death. It is an established fact that Yogis who had cultivated the concept of 'Aloka' or illumination has no reason whatsoever to be perturbed by approaching death. When final moment approaches there would be happiness and contentment. He would be absolutely conscious of the fact that his future re-birth would be in a state that is many many times more propitious than the state in which he is now in and is about to depart. His mind then would become diffused by a sense of perfect calm and bliss.

A virtuous person who had constantly performed positive meritorious deeds would naturally accrue to himself a tremendous amount of positive Karma Vipaka, that would greatly influence and condition his re-linking conciousness or "Pati Sandi Citta" based primarily on the positive and calm Kusal Citta that penetrates his whole being just prior to passing away. There is no doubt whatsoever that a person who has developed transcendental meditation to a great degree, would experience the great illumination that he had already seen during his lifetime while in meditational practices. At the demise of such a noble person there should not be lamentation and weeping, but a state of wise understanding happiness, resulting from understanding the true significance of the change that had occured.

It has to be emphasised that lamentation would have a detrimental effect on all who so lament. This element of sadness is a negative attitude. One weeps pondering on the loss both physical and otherwise that had so occured and thus accrue to oneself a whole range of negative thought process, which invariably fill the mind with darkness and obscures clarity of conception. This situation does not either benefit the one who has departed nor even the one who remains behind. Mind's illumination is lost and darkness takes its place.

CHAPTER XXII

Relatives who often harm the departed

Today's discussion would mainly be on the subject as to what would be the situation that would be prevalent when an individual passes away and finds existence in an intermediate state of 'Antara -Bhava' and the subsequent results arising from outpouring of lamentation of the bereaved relatives and friends.

If a person at the point of death is unable to, whatever reason to acquire a suitable re-birth, then how such a person would enter into an intermediate existence was discussed previously. This temporary state is termed in Pali as a "Gandabba".

Let us recall here a few salient facts for the purpose of clarity. The life breath and consciousness that had been closely associated with fivefold physical body get separated at death. If there be no immediate re-linking of mind leading to renewed existence, then as had been explained earlier the departing consciousness creates for itself a diffused mind-made body almost as a replica of the body left behind at death. At that moment the departing consciousness is not quite aware of the fact that death has really occured. This condition could easily be compared to a dream state. The individual whose merits are of a low order gets somewhat confused. If he had been one who had been very greedily attached to life's conditions, then his consciousness reacts around the dead body being in a way unable to quite detach itself from it. It glances at the dead form that lies in front of him. It sees the dead form. It seens to appreciate the fact its body is in two places. This brings about a condition of confusion. There is an element of disturbance at this stage. The realisation that death has occured is not fully realised. This confusion increases and an element of fears arises when the wailing and lamentation of relatives are heard at this moment. It realises that lamentation is connected with disaster. In these circumstances the feeling of great disaster encompass it fully as it were. This condition of confusion becomes more accelerated to those whose de-merits are more pronounced. At this stage a concept of fear overtakes it. As these impressions come in without any control or discernment the agitation is increased manifold. Then the consciousness that is associated with fine mind made body tries to run away to a distant location. Then from a distance it looks at the dead body, as it is fairly difficult to disassociate itself from the body that it had liked so much.

When the loud lamentation cease somewhat it again cautiously approaches the dead body. This situation can be compared to a dog that had been chased away from the morsel of food by a pelting of stone. When the pelting ceases it again comes cautiously towards the food. If lamentation commences again, it would flee again with added fright. In such a situation, the opportunity for the mind to regain its lustre is completely prevented and becomes diminished. By lustre is meant the force that is generated from meritorious acts of the past. What will come to the fore-front are the dark de-meritorious forces. This darkness is accelerated by the wailing of relatives. What had been discussed here is the conditions that prevail at the demise of an individual whose de-meritorious acts have been very pronounced. Its consciousness is enveloped in darkness.

What is the general and usual form of lamentation adopted by relatives. It usually takes the form of describing the devoted attention adopted by the person when alive towards his kith and kin. When this is heard by the 'Antara-Bhavika' its desire for the just departed life increases. The primary feeling of fear that had earlier arisen, now gradually dissappear, and the departed being gets somewhat used to the condition that is prevalent. It realises the fact that death has now occured. The feeling dawns that if it were to be re-born in another state, then it would be a great loss to its family and children. Its affection and attachment to the family increases. A feeling grows as to how good it would be to live again with its departed family.

If at this state the last departing thoughts get closely impregnated with attachment to the life that had existed prior to death, then the condition can deteriorate very seriously. Such an unfortunate situation would actually arise, if the attachment to family, children and wealth had grown to great proportions. These attachments will naturally be very conducive for the departed to take the form of a low-spirit or what is generally termed by the common people as a 'Mala Perata'. The aforesaid lamentations of relatives would certainly enhance the conditions that would naturally lead to such an unfortunate state.

An unsatisfactory development occurs at this stage. It recognizes its former relatives who had departed earlier and had found existence in such a state. With the recognition there grows an affinity and closeness with these persons departed. The previously departed ones attempt to draw the 'Antara-Bhavike' to their fold. Such getting together is a usual and normal condition of ordinary people when alive. It is a natural tendency that those with similar tendencies would like to group themselves together. The lamentation of relatives and the draw that is exerted by the 'departed petas' on the 'Antara-Bhavika' will form a strong condition for the 'Antara-Bhavika' to find re-birth in such a low depressed state. Now it would be quite evident to the foolish lamenting relatives, what a great dis-service they have done to their departed relative by such lamentation.

What is the next development in the aforesaid process? The consciousness that generally succeed the death moment now draws the 'Antara-Bhavika' towards the Peta-Worlds or such depressed states. I would consider this state as a further strengthening of the mind made body consisting of waves or vibrations. It is so concluded as the body of those in the lower or Peta-Worlds, also consist of fine matter. In this state the individual is transformed into a little more substantial form than the mind made body that consisted of vibrational waves. There is a view among some scientists that there could be very fine physical formations that may not be visible to the naked eye. Our physical eye takes in three diamentional forms or even two diamentional forms of length and breadth. Modern science has concluded that there are other forms consisting of many varied diamentional forms. Experiments about these varied diamentional forms are being carried out at present.

According to Buddhist concept what had happened here is that a helpful or 'Upastambaka Kamma' had influenced the re-establishment or re-birth of the departed consciousness. Because of the great desire or attachment towards worldly goods and wealth that had arisen at the moment of death, it had so determined the last thoughts that he had found re-linking in the 'Peta-World' of depressed states. The wailing relatives had unknowingly as it were assisted towards establishing a helpful 'karma', that had conditioned such low birth. As it is already known an 'Upastambhaka Kamma' or helpful kamma is a meritorious or de-meritorious thought of such action done during lifetime, and which comes foremost to mind at the moment of death and thus being the basis of happiness or unhappiness in the future, then the future existence would definitely be in the very low and painful state of suffering. But in the moment if some effective good kamma influence too comes to the fore-front though born in the 'Peta World' it would cause that existence to be one of great significance; stated in common words it would result in the existence of 'Peta' of a somewhat more powerful composition.

It would now be realised as to how important it would be to avoid unnecessary lamentation at a demise of a relative. Instead it would be very beneficial and helpful to the departing one if those that remain behind were to perform or engage in some religious rite or other on such a significant occasion. Undoubtedly such positive action would act as a helpful 'karmic force' to influence the re-linking consciousness. The 'Antara-Bhavika' would then accrue to itself all these positive meritorius tendencies, as has been explained earlier it would unhesitatingly accept every concept. This is because the feelings to the 'Antara-Bhavika' is very similar to that of a tender child. It is important to realise the fact that although it would be possible to influence and foster the re-linking consciousness, it would not be possible to radically alter or change completely such re-linking consciousness. It is therefore imperative on those that are left behind in this world to act expediously to help an 'Antara-Bhavika' to move away from such a state as soon as possible. Much meritorius activities should be performed on its behalf. As a result of these good deeds performed, even the departing consciousness at death could be so influenced as to obtain 'Pati-Sandhi' or re-linking in a higher plane of existence.

It is the view of Mahayana Teachers, that all beings at death spend some time or other in an intermediate or 'Antara-Bhavika' state. They also accept the view that by the performance of meritorious deeds by others such an 'Antara-Bhavika' could certainly be directed towards liberation or Nirvana.

In my view both these contentions seem to be somewhat erroneous. I have a firm opinion that even if the departing consicousness were to enter into an intermediate state or 'Antara-Bhava' it is not possible for the mind made body in such an aforesaid state to establish such a consciousness strong enough to cause a re-linking or re-birth. The reasons for the above conclusion are as follows:-

It would be easier to accept the conclusion if one were to consider the manner by which Karma and Karma-Vipaka is manifest. It is an established fact, that the mind, the body and speech (sita, kaya, and vachana) are the media through which actions or 'Karma' manifest. It is through the combination of body and mind, or mind and speech combination that actions arise. The results or vipaka manifest through such combination. There is no re-linking force for a Karmic concept that had generated through the mind only, without the active support of the other two doors. The five fold sensual pleasures are felt through the active combination of the two sense doors of mind and body. Taking of life, stealing, drinking intoxicants, engaging in sexual mis-conduct, are all committed through the active collaboration of the body and mind. False speech, harsh speech and tale bearing are committed through the agency body and mind and words. This combination apply for meritorius deeds as well. What is most prominent for a future re-linking process is the Karma-Vipaka that flows for action perfected through the active participation of mind and body or mind and words. These results become prominent at the moment of death, in the form of a 'Janaka Kamma' or re-linking force. It is not possible for the mind alone to generate a 'janaka-kamma' that would cause re-linking or re-birth. An 'antara-bhavika' or being in an intermediate state has mind combined with a finely constituted vibrational body. Through such a weak combination the performance of an active Karma is not possible at all. In such an intermediate state there is no possibility for the accruing of Kamma or even the diminishing of Kamma. In this state only one form of action is possible, and that is to partake of the results of the prevailing perfected Kamma, or actions. As this aspect has been discussed in the earlier chapter there is no need for amplification here.

An individual who had been deeply engrossed in the five-fold sensual pleasures, would find that at the moment of death or departure from life, in such situation thoughts would be very prominent in his consciousness at death. Such thoughts that had continuously and constantly influenced the mind and would naturally come to the fore-front at death, and effectually condition the re-linking or re-birth process.

In what manner does a helpful kamma (Upattambhaka kamma) influence a being in an intermediate or 'antara-bhavika' state. It had been explained earlier that no new actions or kamma are performed in such a state. If there be any meritorious vipaka of kamma or action that had been performed earlier be induced to come to the fore-front, such induced meritorius thoughts would certainly condition and influence the re-linking thought process.

The re-linking thought process would become pure and thus a purified effulgance would arise. If the last thought so influenced be de-meritorius in character then there would arise a film of darkness. Whether it be effulgance or darkness that arise at such a moment, such a background cannot materially alter the place or re-linking or re-birth that had been derived by the 'pati sandhi citta' or re-linking consciousness. What would be certainly influenced by luminosity or darkness of the status in each of these states. If de-meritorius actions had defined that the re-birth as a dog in the animal kingdom, a meritorius thought process at the last stage could not naturally change that animal status, but it could certainly lead for the animal to be born in a wealthy household. It would then be seen that the Mahayana concept that an individual who had continually and consistently performed evil deeds in his lifetime could obtain the bliss of Nibbana by a positive meritorious last thought process, or 'antara bhavika' who is in an intermediate state, by the influence of good deed performed earlier, can attain supreme bliss of Nirvana become quite untenable. The Buddha had emphatically sated that last thought process of a dying individual would condition his re-linking or re-birth. This is the Noble Truth that prevails during all times.

Looking at these problems from another angle could it be stressed that good and meritorious actions that had not been performed by a person in his lifetime could be so completely performed on his behalf by others after his demise. Such a situation is quite impossible. What would be the result of such meritorious actions performed by relatives on behalf of the departed person. The results of such actions can only grant a temporary relief to the departed or somewhat enhance his lowly condition. If the departed being had found existence in tremendously depressed place of suffering, such merit performed would be of no value.

CHAPTER XXIII

The janaka - citta or impulsive thought process that is generated at death caused by a time bomb.

It remains a problem to some as to what would have influenced the last consciousness of an individual who dies suddenly being a casualty at the explosion of a time bomb. This problem could be clarified if one were to ponder as to how a 'Janaka Kamma' or impelling action and its accruing results would condition the re-birth of an individual in a subsequent state.

It is known that Kamma and its results accrue in the consciousness of an individual. As it is generally known there are two varieties of kamma known as Janaka kamma that establish rebirth and the other variety that condition the status of life. This second variety can be classified as all actions both of the negative and positive varieties where vipaka or result is felt by the individual at every stage in his sansaric journey. The degree of happiness and unhappiness, pain and pleasure, is due to the result of this variety of Kamma.

We have heard it said "Oh everything that this man undertakes ends in complete success. It is his previous kamma. How often have I tried to be successful? Everything I undertake end in failure. It is my fate". This sort of comment is made when situations arise which manifestly display the effect of the second variety of kamma described earlier. It is important to consider the fact that what an individual undergoes from the time of his birth to the time of his death is directly considered and influenced by the effect of his action, both of the present and past. By a 'Janaka Kamma' is meant a force that comes to the forefront at the moment of death and that which condition the next life. This kamma also determines the state whether human Deva or animal etc. in which the departing individual would find re-birth. It certainly determines the future state of an individual and hence can be considered as very vital and important.

When the eye sees a form, the conclusion can be arrived at that such form is beautiful and pleasant. It is similar with the other sense doors as well. But these impressions that are taken in by the sense doors, do not condition the re-link process or re-birth. It has been so stated by the Buddha. "Panchadhvarika kamman patisandhe nibbthtakan na-hoti pavatti vipakan pana deti".

Then what would condition the re-birth kamma? It is when any impression taken in by the five sense doors transfer themselves into a 'kamma-Patha' or course of action that could both he wholesome or unwholesome, that would ultimately become a Janaka kamma that would condition re-birth. "Tatta Patisandi Nibbathika Kama Patha-patava Dattabban". It is these that have been transferred into a kamma-patta or course of action that really become kamma. Any action that would accrue to itself completely, all such essential features would naturally become a course of action or 'kamma - patha'.

Let us now consider the evil action of the deprivation of an animal's life or killing. It is generally known there are five conditions that should be fulfilled to fully constitute the act of killing. The first should be the sentient being that would die, that such is a sentient being, followed by the desire to kill, then the adoption of the means to kill and finally the act of killing. If the above five conditions are not completed it would not constitute the evil act of killing. An accidental death of a sentient creature would certainly not constitute the evil act of killing with its final evil results. If with the idea of chasing away an animal an instrument is used for such chasing and unfortunately that instrument hits the animal at a vital place and death occurs, such an action does not constitute the act of killing. This is so because there was no intention to kill. The only necessity there was to chase the animal away.

It would now become quite clear that what transfers itself into a 'Janaka-Kamma' are those actions that have been done with careful pre-meditation and thought. Thoughts of such deeds are well embedded in the mind. These can be compared to fertile seeds that are well planted in the soil and with the addition of moisture the seeds sprout up as plants. Such deeds performed consistently get impregnated deeply in the mind and consciousness. It is like residue that have settled at the bottom. It is quite possible that such residue impregnates, and may implant itself in the deep recesses of the mind and rise up when occasion so demands. This state would be completely eliminated when the mind has reached higher transcendental states. A consequential Karma can give results at any stage, but this sort of Karma has no power to change the state or condition of existence.

By the frequent performance of positive and meritorious action the results of past evil proclivities may certainly be reduced and diminished. Who could correctly surmise the amount of meritorious or demeritorious action performed by an individual in its immensly long sansaric journey. Even if one were to examine one life span the good and bad performed would be quite immeasurable.

In the world there are more opportunities for evil actions than good and wholesome ones. According to environmental conditions of life, good and bad become manifest. If for some Karmic reason or other an individual is born among those of criminal tendencies, then the opportunity to perform good deeds would be greatly diminished. To what extent are we aware of the quantities of residual karma that is deposited at the base of our minds. These 'anushaya' characteristics may rise up at any opportune moment. It is very cogent to think deep on these matters and cultivate thoughts that invariably lead towards emancipation.

It looks as if we had commenced to speak on re-linking or re-birth and diverted on to another topic. Yet at this moment it would not be inappropriate to somewhat ponder on what has been said earlier.

Let us imagine a situation where an individual had been caught in the midst of an exploding time bomb and had died instantly. Let us imagine the situation where at such a time of disaster, many had been reduced to ashes. Would it have been possible a person in such a situation to develop a flow of consciousness of a departing mind that would lead to re-linking or re-birth. It would be quite possible for such an individual to have been considering as to what he would do on the following day in office or some such similar thought process. Would such a thought process be strong enough to establish the re-linking process. It would therefore be not incorrect to consider the fact that an intermediate or 'Antara-Bhavika' state would be helpful to the person who had just died. If there had been no such re-linking thought process at death, till such time such a re-birth thought process would suitably arise, it would become invariably necessary for the dead individual to spend some period of time, though temporarily in a state termed as an 'antara-bhava'. I hold the view that the reference to a final thought process that influences and conditions the re-linking process explained in the Buddhist doctrine refer to deaths that occur in the normal process, where there is ample opportunity for the arising of such a thought process. I have not seen or read in any context in the Buddha-Dhamma, where the Lord had stated that a person would not die without the establishment of the 'Janaka Kamma' force, that conditions the re-link process. If there be no such reference as assumed by me, what would then be the situation as would result in the case of the exploding time bomb?

According to the activities that had been performed when living and as a result of such activities, as if almost unknown to him, the last thought process may arise. To explain this further, at the very moment consciousness leaves the body according to Karmic Laws, a meritorious or demeritorious resulting or Vipaka thought could arise. Conditioned by such a background the re-linking thought process may arise, leading to a re-establishment or re-birth. It certainly is not possible in such an instant to decide that the dying individual would breathe his last, seeing signs and sights in his sub-conscious mind of the places of his future re-birth (Gati Nimiti).

It had been said that the fly on an anvil, as the hammer comes down and swaps its life away there would arise the last thought process. The condition of mind change and alter many thousands of times in the brief space of a moment and the succeeding state would arise according to the prevailing consciousness at that moment.

Beings roam in the wide samsaric ocean because of the immense degree of greed or 'tanha'. We are aware that this 'tanha' or craving is three-fold: viz. the craving for worldly sense pleasures, desire or craving for existence, and the craving for anihiliation or non-existence. The craving for worldly sense pleasures demands desire for a pleasure and comfortable life conditions bereft of suffering and discomfort. The craving for existence displays a desire to enjoy this pleasure in a continuous unbroken fashion. It is due to this concept of craving that the Nirvanic Ideal gets further and further away from their minds. An individual has a continuous experience of enjoying the fivefold sense pleasures. To an ordinary uninitiated mind the Nirvanic concepts and ideals are further away from them and one so foreign to them. To a mind where worldly comforts and ideas have got strongly embedded such concepts regarding Nibbana would be of little use. The search is accentuated towards worldly pleasures.

The general wish of many individuals, who perform acts of merit like 'Dana' or liberality, is to obtain heavenly happiness or earthly happiness consequent to such actions and then afterwards, finally obtain the Bliss of Nirvana. The Nirvana state is ironically delayed and pushed to the last. The ordinary mind always craves for happiness and physical comforts. Even at the dying moment the craving or desire is for the enjoyment of heavenly pleasures even for a brief span of a day.

This condition is manifest consequent to the manner in which we have fashioned and trained our minds. Mind's usual characteristic is craving and hence clinging or attachment is very strong. Craving is like stretching forth of a hand towards an object. Attachment is akin to tight grasping of a object without letting it go. It is the force of getting together or gathering together that is prevalent here. This gathering together or getting together is none other than the powerful Karmic force. Even if one was to pass away in the absence of a Janaka thought process, yet it is important to remember that the Karmic force is ever present. It has to be stated emphatically that even if death occurs consciously or unconsciously or if death occurs knowingly or unknowingly the Karmic force that is embedded in the mind does not get destroyed or eliminated even by a minutest degree.

On such an occasion as a sudden or unexpected death, that occurs instantly as it were the consciousness that establishes itself in an intermediate state of 'antara-bhava' would be in somewhat disturbed condition. It may not fully comprehend as to what had really happened. There would certainly be a state of shock, but with almost no pain as such. For the pain to become manifest there should have been some aspect of time, which is completely absent in this situation. When I questioned many who had met with sudden accidents, lost consciousness. but later when regained consciousness, they all expressed the view, that they did not remember or comprehend what had happened. They specifically stated that they had not experienced any painful feeling. They had become unconscious immediately with the impact. They had realised as to what had happened only after they had regained consciousness.

From this it would become manifestly clear that a person dying in such circumstances would not have the time to experience any painful feelings. The question has to be asked whether the consciousness that had entered this intermediate state would remain in this "gandabba form" for ever as it were.

As had been explained earlier even when in this intermediate state, there would flow into the consciousness, the remembrance of good and bad actions done previously. There would appear a concept of effulgence or darkness as the case may be. Those who have cultivated the concept of light would follow the path of effulgence and take re-birth in a place of happiness. Those that follow the path of darkness as suits their previous deed would follow the path of murky darkness and be re-born in places of distress and sorrow.

If would thus be seen, that to be re-born in a subsequent state of existence, the last Janaka or impelling thoughts do not directly influence such re-birth. It may be that the re-linking thought process may arise in the intermediate or Antara-Bhava' state. The method of the arising of these last thoughts in the 'antara-bhava' are very similar to the process as to how it would arise at the point of a normal death. Therefore if there be a very forceful or "Garuka Kamma" that would take precedence over all others and come to the forefront. The most heinous actions that give immediate results or vipaka are matricide, patricide, causing schism in the Sangha, and such others. A person who had committed such crimes, would naturally be re-born in the worst form of hellish existence termed as the 'Avichi Maha Narakaya'. Those who adhere to very rigid false views would also be subjected to great pain and distress in the future birth. Taking into consideration the enormous amount of crime perpetuated in the present day, it would be quite useful to ponder on this matter in a somewhat detailed manner. They are as follows. There is the view that liberality is of no value. There is no consequent result arising from meritorious or demeritorious deeds. There is no beyond to those of the present world. There is no result accruing from looking after mother or father affectionately or even non-affectionately. There is no well established Sangha and devoted Monks. There are no beings that are re-born after death.

Those who stubbornly adhere to such concepts would certainly find re-birth in places of great distress and sorrow. Why is it that they are re-born in such misery? This awful condition arises because of the fact that those with such stubborn ideas, have no desire or inclination towards the performance of good and benevolent deeds. They could commit any crime with impunity. Those who have accrued to themselves great wealth through foul and illegal means get engrossed in the five-fold sense pleasures in an unlimited and extreme fashion. It would thus be seen that there is no other suitable place for their future existence other then the "Avichi Narakaya". Their deeds while living have been of such hideous nature, that there is no alternative but these awful places of distress for them.

This indicates clearly, that if there be a very powerful Kamma either of the positive or negative variety, that powerful Kamma always take precedence over all others and transfers itself into a Janaka or generative kamma and determine the next existence. If there be no such forceful kamma, then the results of action done in a proximate manner come forward and condition the next birth. Proximate means in proximately to death. Such action would certainly condition the next life when death occurs in a normal and usual manner.

In the case of a sudden death as discussed earlier, there is no time factor available for a proximate kamma to make its presence felt. But it is important to realize that such a thought process can be induced by those that have been left behind. This is a great service that they could render to those that are departed.

If at the moment of death there had been no possibility for the establishment of some thought process, then it would be correct to assume that a re-linking thought process could be established in the intermediate or 'antara-bhavika' state a very potential 'Garuka Kamma' or weighty Kamma would appear at first. This aspect had been, described earlier. Next in order would be an 'Assana-Kamma' or 'Achinna Kamma' or a stored up 'Katakka Kamma'. would act as the re-linking force. It would be worthwhile to pay some attention to consider how the mind reacts at such a moment.

It is not possible to determine the beginings of this long Sansaric journey. It is safe to assume that this enormously long journey would consist of manifold aeons. It is safe to assume that the results of the positive and negative actions are not all deposited in the mind or consciousness. Most of these Kammas world have become exhausted after their results or vipaka had been experienced at some time or other in the Sansaric journey. But it is possible that those who have committed habitual serious de-meritorious actions, would find their effects as it were deposited in the base of the consciousness as a form of silt.

In the Buddha Dhamma this so called silt is termed as "Anusaya" and can be termed as latent proclivities, inclinations or tendencies that are deposited deeply in the mind. The quantum of the good and bad performed and what the deposits are that are embedded, are not known. It had been explained earlier that the mind or consciousness moves in a circular fashion. Yet I have a firm conviction that consciousness or mind itself is spherical. This is so because that mind's activities occur according to universal laws. The meritorious and demeritorious Kamma accrue therein. A yogi who had deligently practiced meditation would be able to clearly decide the state of the mind. Further a Yogi who has awakened the "Kudalini" would be able to observe very clearly the working of the mind. To such a Yogi the movement of the mind would be akin to the slow movement of a serpent around all the sides of a spherical object. The movement of the mind around the varied surface of a spherical object could be clearly discernable.

Where de-meritorious thoughts occupy the mind, then there is a tendency for the mind to shrink around those thought processes. There would be a diminishing in its size. At times of meditational exercises the mind would expand and spread around. When de-meritorious thoughts and evil proclivities have been eliminated, then the mind expands and becomes one with infinity. It was because of this condition that the Buddha classified Nirvana as infinite, and limitless. There is a limit to the mind when it is narrowed down owing to the evil proclivities that are constantly present.

In order to understand this concept let us place a black spot on the surface of a balloon. When the balloon is gradually inflated the black spot would expand and as the surface of the balloon expands to such an extent that it would almost disappear from sight. When the balloon is deflated, the black spot would again become visible.

When the mind expands at times of meditation a similar situation would occur to the evil proclivities that had been embedded in the mind. Evil proclivities can be equated with darkness. When the mind expands in meditation the dark evil conditions would get dissolved and finally disappear.

When such expansions occur there would not be the possibility even for strongly embedded evil tracts to remain unchanged. Like a balloon it is not positive to expand it up to a certain point and then stop expansion. Through meditation it could be possible to expand the mind to limitless infinity. As the mind expands it would not be possible to keep it enclosed within a certain limit and make it expand no further. It is because of this important factor that a person who has gained the knowledge towards expansion of the mind, would never become mentally ill. In such expansion the individual would be able to reach from stage to stage transcendental qualities, which would lead finally towards mind's emancipation and finally reach the end of the samsaric journey. To those who have got used to develop their minds according to the teaching of Buddhism entertain no doubts regarding the Noble Doctrine. I tried to explain this aspect in somewhat simple and detailed manner in order to show how meritorious and de-meritorious proclivities had been collected in the mind, displaying both positive and negative characteristics.

It is important to realise the fact that resultant vipaka accruing from any action depend on the gravity of the action concerned. Even in the act of killing there are different levels of gravity. The five henious crimes discribed earlier are considered 'anantariya kamma', resulting in immediate destiny in hellish suffering. The vipaka accruing from the act of killing vary according to the degree of seriousness of the crime perpetrated.

Even the act of killing the consequent results vary according to the seriousness implied in such an act. There certainly is difference in an act that snuffs out the life of a human being when compared to the killing of an animal or the killing of an insect like a mosquito. The degree of seriousness in each of these vary according to the gravity of the deed. Even in the meritorious act of giving of alms, the degree of benefits change according to the personality of the recipient. Alms given to a begger would certainly bear great results. But alms offered to a righteous Bhikku would result in greater benefit to the donor.

Alms offered to an Arahant would be of much greater consequence and alms offered to Buddha, would be of limitless merit. It would thus be noticed that there is a degree of variance. The impressions imprinted in the mind also vary accordingly.

If at the moment of death there is no impelling or Javana Citta present then in the intermediate 'antara-bhave' state a meritorious or de-meritorious thought process would come to the forefront according to the degree of strength of each thought process. Otherwise the remembrance on a act of a serious nature, perpetrated even a few days prior to death would come to the fore-front. It may also be possible for the remembrance of a very powerful meritorious act engaged in close proximity to death would take precedence. It is quite evident that what had been done recently remains fresh in the memmory, than what had been done in the distant past. If there be some act that had resulted in creating a very deep impression accompanied by almost convulsive shock, such incidents will be deeply laid in the mind, would naturally come to the fore-front at death. Such impressions would become active and prominent even in the intermediate 'antara-bhava' state. Such a condition cannot become manifest if a person were to pass away in an unexpected moment as the sudden explosion of a time bomb.

As there are no physical sense faculties to a being in the intermediate state (antara-bhava) the previously performed meritorious and de-meritorious actions re-coil on the consciousness at lightening speed. There would be a sudden uprising of darkness and fear consequent to dark deeds previously done. When the results of meritorious deeds appear, there would be a halo of light, a sense of happiness and contentment. There would be a great sense of satisfaction and calm. This intensity is because of the fact that such feeling is felt directly by the consciousness and not controlled through the agency of the five-fold sense faculties. As illustrating this condition, reflecting an occasion when living when an unfounded fear or unfounded happiness may have influenced and percolated into your mind. The feeling that an 'antara-bhavika' would experience would be many hundred times more intense than the above situation. As said earlier this intensity and exaggeration of both happiness and suffering is due to the absence of the five-fold senses that exert a controlling influence on sense impressions. This aspect of the working of the consciousness in the above intermediate state can be well understood, by those who had somewhat perfected meditational practices. What is attempted in meditational exercises is to cut off the influence of the five-fold senses or the consciousness, and to make it concentrated on a single topic. The attempt is to concentrate the mind on a single topic, cutting away the tendency for it to diffuse or spread about, into other areas.

When the mind is so concentrated or 'citta ekaggata' is reached, even a small sound would be felt with some intensity. The sound would be felt with a greater sense of intensity. Similarly even the satisfaction that one derives from the stilling of the mind in meditation would thus be greatly en-hanced. This is due to the fact that the influence exerted by the five sense doors has been temporarily suppressed. This state of the mind can be correctly appreciated by one engaged in meditational practices. It would then become very clear how impressions come flowing in without any control or opposition.

When meditational exercises are commenced at first, a beginner would experience a situation where he would visualise somewhat fearful and frightening sights. There would be occasions that a beginner would see mentally fearful aspects of Titians or Nagas, or even skeletons, great openings of darkness. There would also be mental sights of halos of light, rows of lamps lotus flowers, garlands and festoons, stars, Devas and images of the Buddha. These would be pleasant sights. All these sights both pleasant and fearful, are not those that come from outside but are the results of impressions that have been in the mind or consciousness earlier.

What is interesting to note is the fact that in the intermediate or 'antara-bhava' state, as the mind is free from the control of five senses both meritorious and de-meritorious impressions come to the fore-front forcefully trying to jostle each other as it were. A worldling when alive would have committed both good and bad. Hence it becomes imperative on those who are yet alive to make every effort to help, the being in the intermediate state to free itself from such a state as quickly as possible.

CHAPTER XXIV

The Antara - Bhavika who drift towards animal existence while in sight of the hellish regions

The above is a topic that needs some further clarification. It would have become clear to the reader by now, that the re-linking thought process just prior to death is according to the good and bad deeds performed when alive. This would naturally include all activities that had been performed during the long sansaric journey. These are the tendencies that have been gathered together during the immense courses of time. An individual's thought process and manner of thinking have all been conditioned to a very great extent according to the inclinations that have been fostered all along. For a person who has criminal tendencies it would be quite natural for him to be absorbed in thoughts pertaining to the evil deeds that have been continually performed by him. Such evil thoughts would not arise in the mind of an individual whose inclinations and tendencies have been always characterised by positive and noble thoughts.

At this stage I would like to discuss as to who constitutes a real Buddhist. Could that person be classified as a Buddhist whose Birth Certificate indicates that he is a Buddhist. It is not difficult to explain who really is a Buddhist, if one were to clearly understand the correct Buddhist concepts. Buddhism leads finally to the realisation of Nibbana or Final emancipation of the mind. Buddhism differs from other religions in the manner of its explanation as to the attainment of final liberation.

It is possible for those yet alive to help those who have passed away giving an opportunity for the arising of a Janaka thought process, so that by such assistance those so departed may find re-birth in a satisfactory place. As such a person who had died before he had the opportunity of establishing a 'Janaka Kamma' that would condition the next birth, may certainly be in such a process.

Good deeds done by the relatives on behalf of the departed can always lead to the enhancement of meritorious thoughts in the consciousness of the departed. It would thus assist him to proceed along the illuminated path. Engaging in positive actions by the relatives in the manner of recital of pirith, reading of religious texts, by the offering of alms, by discussing about the positive good deeds performed by the departed relative, can certainly assist in the dawning of meritorious thought process in the consciousness of the 'Antara Bhavika' that would ultimately lead him to a fortunate re-linking process or 'pati sandi' and re-birth. Such actions can be far more benefical than mere lamentation and the negative process of shedding of tears. If those that are left behind get drunk to full capacity, and commence reading books aloud in some awful fashion that would even disturb the minds that are around them it would be quite natural for the departed 'antara-bhavika' to get more confused and disturbed, that would drive him to re-establish himself in places of distress and suffering. The elders of the household should strictly prohibit the use of alcohol and such practices in a house that had experienced some bereavement. When groups get together in such a house and engage themselves in bouts of drinking and card playing, if the departed 'antara-bhavika' had been addicted to liquor when alive then it would naturally get attracted to such company, Naturally enjoy the liquor and so enhance its negative characteristics further. If the departed had been one who had abhored strong drinks, then seeing such a situation it would cause it consciousness to get disturbed and distracted. What would have happened on both these instances is for the prevention, and laying serious obstacles for the one departed to be re-born in a place of happiness and well-being. If those in the bereaved household would get together and perform such religious activities on behalf of the one so departed, there could be no better noble practice and noble action that could be done. Such actions would be condusive for the establishment of solace and harmony among those that are alive, and certainly would open up greater opportunity for the departed to be re-born in a place of happiness and bliss.

    The Buddhist way of life excludes evil action and development of all positive traits. If this be the only ideal in the Buddhist doctrine, then there would be not much difference between Buddhism and other religions philosaphies. But it is important to consider the fact that the final aim of other religions are heaven or 'Moksha' is basically different from the concept of Nirvana or total emancipation. Buddhism leads to the final goal of Nirvana. A Buddhist is an individual who shapes and fashions his life towards reaching the final goal of Nirvana or liberation. I wonder how many so called Buddhists in this country conform to the above ideal? How many fashion their lives in such a manner to reach this ideal condition? An individual whose ideal is Nirvana should so fashion and shape his mind towards this final goal. This ideal if not reached in one's present life span, can be targetted for even a future life. The training and shaping of the mind can be achieved only through a process of Meditation or 'Bhavana'. The mind should be so cultivated as the realisation of Nirvana, can occur only through the mind. An individual who constantly engages in meditational practices, can immediately recognise a negative thought process that had so entered the mind. There would be the immediate recognition of an evil or beneficial thought process. A person whose mind had been so developed through meditational practices would be able not only to recognise such thoughts, but also to estimate the harm that accrue from such a negative thought process. He would therefore make every effort to protect his well guarded mind and free it from the pernicious effects of an evil thought process. If the attaiment of Nirvana is his ideal he would realise the fact that enhancing such evil thoughts would be quite detrimental for the realisation, of this noble ideal. Elimination of all evil proclivities, elimination of greed or 'tanha' and complete elimination of state of 'Upadana' or binding would be characteristic of the absolute peaceful state of the Nirvanic mind.

To an individual whose ideal is the attainment of Nirvana either in this lifetime or in the future, would not wish to entertain and establish evil thoughts in his mind. Even if it may not be quite possible for him to prevent the influence of such thoughts, yet he would make every effort to prevent them from being established totally in the mind. He would recognise such a thought, realise its evil nature and try to dispel it as quickly as possible. He would question himself how it would be possible for him to attain such a noble and peaceful state if he entertains and fosters such negative thought processes. If he had practiced mind cultivation or the basis of contemplating or the noble qualities of the Buddha, he would constantly concentrate on those noble qualities and despise the evil thought process that had arisen and try to establish a protective shield as it were against such evil tendencies. He would visualise the Buddha through his mental eye. Every attempt would be made by him to shape his mind on the basis of the noble qualities of the Buddha. He would attempt to understand the transitiveness that is manifest and thus protect his mind.

It would be useful to consider as to how one would re-act when a negative thought process enter ones mind. Do you exert sufficiently to protect your mind from evil results that may accrue or would you allow that negative thought process to establish itself firmly in the mind, and to shape your activities in accordance with that evil thought process. In this situation if you act in the way I had described earlier, then you can be classified as a true Buddhist. If the answer is otherwise, then you are only a nominal Buddhist. You are a Buddhist to the extent you satisfy the requirements of the Birth Certificate. No more. You will not be able to reach the further boundaries of emancipation. Nirvana is very distant to you.

I explained this situation in somewhat great detail in order to stress as to how evil proclivities arise and how the mind can be protected from such tendencies. I was on the subject of the last thoughts of the dying individual. I digressed somewhat because I am aware that to the ordinary uninitiated mind, contemplation on death and dying really do not seep deep down into the mind.

If thoughts flow into the mind in the manner described, the question would arise whether it would be possible for us to effectually dispel a thought process that had so arisen. It can only be stated that thought process often arise in the mind in accordance with the manner in which the mind had been cultivated. At the moment of death would it be possible to establish the re-linking or re-birth process, in accordance with one's own wishes or aspirations. It would be correct to assume that the opportunity for an arising of a positive thought process to one who has performed good deeds, would certainly be more pronounced. Let us consider as to what would be the last thought process for a person who had committed much crime. The classical explanation is as follows: Craving (tanha) leads to clinging (upadana) which leads on to the process of becoming (bhava) which lead on to re-birth (jati). This is the process that leads to re-becoming or re-birth. Tanha in the above context refers to the persistent desire to find existence over and over again and enjoy the pleasures derived from the fivefold sense impressions. As long as this desire remains embedded in the consciousness of an individual there can never be a final stop to the sansaric journey. Tanha can be akin to great drawing togetherness. It is like the attraction exerted by a magnet. It is a desire to get pushed forwards. This desire impels the further extension of the sansaric journey. It does not indicate any wish towards the conclusion of this journey. The term 'upadana' can be termed as clinging together. It is akin to the situation that exist when iron gets attracted towards a magnet.

The force or energy that together is provided by Karma, had been accrued from age to age. This Karmic force acts in the same way as fuel provides the engine for its forward push. In this instance it provides the so called 'fuel' for re-becoming or re-birth in whatever state. It pushes the mind forward. It must ever go forward. It cannot stop or cease to push forward. Even if there be the desire to halt, it cannot do so as it is akin to a vehicle without brakes. Now let us imagine that at the moment of death, according to deeds performed earlier, a Janaka or determining Kamma arises that would condition re-birth in the animal state. In such a situation it would not be possible for it to make a choice and say "I do not desire to take re-birth in the animal state" and thus stay back in the 'antara-bhava' state. Whether one likes it or not this movement towards the animal state cannot be averted. This journey should necessarily take place as the force for such a journey had been provided by Karma-Vipaka. If a person is on the brink of a great abyss and is about to fall in, such a desperate moment would arise at such a time. In order to avoid the fall whatever that comes in hand should be grasped. This would be similar to the situation when a drowning individual would even grab at a strand of straw, in order to avoid the impending disaster.

To a criminal who had entered the intermediate state of Existence, the thoughts and impressions that flow towards him can be compared to one who is about to fall into an abyss of darkness. In such a state those emotions flow in unimpelled, and the remembrance of past misdeeds and crimes come in with a tremendous force. The characteristics of such feelings are mainly of fear a sense of torture and incessant burning. To such a person who is about to fall into a perpetual fire of molten lava, the animal world of existence could be compared to a heavenly realm.

If it be possible in the minutest way to avoid the above disaster, he would immediately clutch at the animal existence. The intense clinging towards such a re-birth would then arise. Even with or without a backward clinging, an inexorable push towards 'Avichi' or the most frightful nether or infernal world occur due to the consequential result of the performance of hedious crime. It is like a determined push across the edge of the deep cliff. Where such a forward push becomes manifest the desire to draw back would be quite futile. The draw back would on the contrary provide further incentives for the forward lurch. In such an instance every attempt to resist the fall-over would be quite useless. To one who has habitually performed negative and de-meritorious acts, the existence in an intermediate state or 'antara-bhava' can prove to be a vertible cauldron of molten liquid. To such it is a place of darkness. It is a place of great torture, and suffering. Even to an individual who had fostered and developed meritorious traits of character, the 'antara-bhava' would certainly not be an environment to tarry long. Even to one with such a cultivated personality there may have been occasions where some evil deeds had been perpetrated. Further it could not be known for certain what type of evil deeds may have been executed in the previous births or existence. It would therefore be seen that in an intermediate state or 'antara-bhava' the results of previous good and bad actions will come forward with a tremendous force. Whatever feeling there be, will be felt very intensely.

It therefore becomes the unbounded duty of those who are yet alive, to make every effort to help in releasing their loved relatives who may have entered into an 'antara-bhavika' state. This release can be hastened by the performance of meritorious deeds on their behalf. When meritorious actions are regularly performed on behalf of the departed, it would cause the increase in volumes of the effulgent side and thus quite enhance the feeling of happiness and well being. Then the perception regarding the place of re-birth would be felt very clearly, and the 'antara-bhavika' would naturally move towards that happy state.

Before I conclude this article today I think it would be apt to disclose an incident that occured when I was attached to the Editorial Staff of the Astrological Paper 'Suba-Setha'. During that time I was privileged to associate closely with the distinguished Literary Scholar Arisen Ahubudu. I was able to come in contact with a friend of his: Mr. Jinadasa Liyanage who was then on the tutorial staff of S. Thomas College, Mount Lavinia. During that period Mr. Jinadasa Liyanage was subjected to a severe heart attack and after being admitted to the Cardiology Unit had then almost passed away. That incident which was later described to me by Mr. Jinadasa Liyanage himself is as follows:- This story provides an interesting background as to what had been explained earlier in these pages. When the heart attack had become very severe, the heart's movement had stopped. Then the doctors and nurses who were around his bed at that time had made every attempt to re-vive the heart's working. Heart massage was adopted and even an electric shock wave was attempted to revive the heart. Every attempt was made expeditiously to bring him back to life. At this moment a strange thing had happened to him. He had felt that as it were he was forcing himself out through a tunnel. He had felt a sense of shock when he came out of the tunnel. He had a feeling as if he was floating upwards towards the ceiling. He was able to observe how the nurses and doctors were attending on him. As he floated out of the room he was also able to see his anxious and worried relations waiting in the corridor of the hospital. He clearly remembers seeing another doctor rushing to his bed-side. While he was experiencing these, he was able to see a great halo of light. He was instantly drawn towards that light. He had never seen such luminosity ever in his life time. He felt a tremendous desire to enter the area of light. As he was attempting to enter into the halo, he felt he experienced a determined feeling which seems to say, "Go back, you have more time to come here". He could not possibly act against that feeling or order. He turned back and floated towards the hospital and looked from above at his body that lay on the bed. As he looked at his own body there was a great dislike for it, as he was so engrossly enchanted with the halo that he had experienced. Yet he felt an impelling order as it were to enter his body. Once again he felt that he was gradually floating back towards his body and entering it. At that moment he heard with his physical ear the verbal expression of the doctors and nurses that all was well and that the crisis had passed. When he once again opened his eyes he saw that the doctors were attending on him diligently.

When Mr. Jinadasa Liyanage related to me his strange experience, I was able to check up the details of his story with the records at the Hospital. I was able to trace the records and meet the Doctors and nurses who had attended on him, at that time. From what they said he had died clinically, but with great effort they had been able to revive him.

Mr. Liyanage when he left hospital had been strictly advised to avoid heavy smoking. But it was strange that he persisted in being a very heavy smoker. When I too advised him to avoid smoking, he remarked that now he was not afraid to die, and that he knew pretty well where he would re-establish himself after death. As a matter of fact he was eagerly awaiting the final hour. Six months after this incident he went on his final journey. As to the place of his destination there cannot be any semblance of doubt.

I would like to mention about the case of the late Mr. Peramunetillake for whom I had a great affection and regard during the time that we were on the Editorial staff of the "Dinamina". It is with deep affection and gratitude that I remember the services he rendered me when I was hospitalised. He had a very compassionate heart that impelled to help those who were in want and distress. His passing away occured when he had visited the temple on his birthday. On that occasion when the Maha Sangha was chanting Pirith, he had breathed his last. According to the teachings of Buddhism, I have no doubt whatsoever that he would have found a re-birth in circumstances far more propitious, where he would be surrounded by great comfort and happiness. We are really comforted by such a thought. But there is a poingnancy felt when we consider as to how early he has left us. He was akin to a fragrant flower among us journalists. I would unhesitatantly wish him the Bliss of Nibbana.